Social Group Work:
We are all in the same boat

Proceedings of the XXXIII International Symposium
on Social Work with Groups
Long Beach, California, USA, June 2-5, 2011

Social Group Work:
We are all in the same boat

Edited by

Cheryl D. Lee

w&b

MMXIV

© Whiting & Birch Ltd 2014
Published by Whiting & Birch Ltd,
Forest Hill, London SE23 3HZ

ISBN 9781861771360

Printed in England and the United States by Lightning Source

CONTENTS

Acknowledgements

Association for the Advancement of Social Work with Groups
XXXIII Annual International Symposium
Long Beach, California, June 2-5, 2011

Symposium Planning Committee
Cheryl D. Lee, Symposium Chair
Vanessa Treadway, Symposium Co-Chair
Maria Gurrola, Symposium Co-Chair
Charisa Ready, Volunteer Coordinator
Marian Klemek
Joy Rubin
Marilyn Potts
Eileen Litchfield
Amanda Sanchez
Zvi Plotnik
Paola Schenkelberg
Maria Gandarilla
Leticia Alvarez
Paul Flory-Duncan
Ally Leff
Ahmed Alsadiq

Symposium IASWG Honorees
Mark Doel
Alex Gitterman

Symposium Local Honorees
Bob Cabeza, VP of Community Development, YMCA, Greater Long Beach
Dean Marilyn Flynn, University of Southern California, School of Social Work
Cheryl D. Lee, IASWG Symposium Chair and S. California Chapter Chair
Dean Kenneth I. Millar, California State University, Long Beach, College of Health and Human Services

Many people and organizations played a role in creation of the Long Beach International Association for Social Work with Groups (IASWG) Symposium Proceedings. Firstly, I would like to thank IASWG without which there would not have been a XXXIII Annual Symposium where social group workers gather from around the world to celebrate social group work and share information and friendship. Steve Kraft was the

President of IASWG during the Long Beach International Symposium which was held aboard the Queen Mary. He did a lot to assist our local planning committee in creating a successful symposium. His knowledge of law greatly assisted IASWG in negotiating a good contract with the Queen Mary. In addition, IASWG Executive Board Members Dominique Steinberg and Nancy Sullivan advised our local planning group and answered our questions through teleconference meetings. Greg Tully, the current IASWG President, was always there to answer questions I had while creating the Proceedings. California State University, School of Social Work and the College of Health and Human Services under Dean Ken Millar, gave great support and resources.

The local symposium planning committee met bi-weekly for a year to plan the symposium, invite presenters, prepare the program, raise funds and do the monumental work behind the scenes of putting on an international symposium. Especially helpful in this endeavor were Vanessa Treadway and Maria Gurrola, the Co-chairs. Vanessa also secured the Queen Mary Photo for our Proceedings cover.

THANK YOU to the contributors to the Proceedings who not only presented great keynotes, papers and workshops at the symposium, but then turned their work into documents which could be published.

The reviewers who read, rated and commented on manuscripts are so appreciated. They shall go unnamed to protect the blind review process but their work greatly assisted the editing.

Ms. Tiffany Lynn, a California State University MSW student volunteered her time to work on the Proceedings. Formerly she had edited a forestry service journal at Yale and her editorial knowledge was invaluable in moving this project forward. I will miss our Friday night editing sessions. This smart woman who comes from Taiwan felt that she learned a lot about social group work from reading the Proceeding manuscripts.

Our publisher, David Whiting and the staff at Whiting and Birch are appreciated for taking the components of the *Proceedings* and magically turning them into a beautiful and meaningful book.

Last but not least, I would like to thank Zvi Plotnik, who is a wonderful and caring partner, in all of my endeavors including the IASWG Long Beach Symposium and Proceedings.

Cheryl D. Lee
Editor

Dedication

The Long Beach IASWG Symposium Proceedings is dedicated to three individuals. They are: Steve Kraft, Zvi Plotnik, and the late Ernest Gunderson.

Mr. Steven Kraft was the President of IASWG during the time of the Long Beach IASWG Symposium's planning and execution. He always was there to lend a hand to our Planning Committee in order to move the Symposium forward. He even attended our local meetings in California while living in New York. His great sense of humor, relaxed approach, knowledge of what is important, and passion for social group work made the IASWG Symposium and *Proceedings* projects enjoyable and meaningful endeavors.

The second dedication is to Mr. Zvi Plotnik. He is an outstanding life partner who unselfishly supported me while I worked full time as a university professor, chaired the international IASWG symposium, edited the IASWG Proceedings, and was a caring family member.

The third dedication is to Ernest Gunderson, an engineer turned social worker, who writes beautifully about men's support groups in the *Proceedings*. He died of cancer a few days after his manuscript was accepted. His untimely death inspired me to finally finish this project with the hope that it would have meaning to his family, group work members and group work learners around the world.

Cheryl D. Lee
Editor

About the Editor

Cheryl D. Lee, PhD, MSW, is Professor of Social Work at California State University, Long Beach (CSULB). She received a BA degree in sociology from George Washington University in Washington, DC, and graduate degrees, MSW and Ph.D., from Arizona State University, School of Social Work. She teaches social group work, human behavior in the social environment, thesis research and field seminar. She started a social group work club for students and practitioners. The popularity of the club was a catalyst for the Southern California (CA) Chapter of IASWG moving its headquarters to Long Beach, California. For many years, she served as Chair of the IASWG Southern CA Chapter and is on its Board of Directors. She served on IASWG's International Board. She was Chair of the 2011 Long Beach IASWG Symposium held on the historic Queen Mary ship. She's been a faculty mentor to many first generation college students. One of these mentees is Vanessa Treadway, BASW, MSW who is the current Chair of the IASWG Southern CA Chapter. She serves on CSULB's Disability Students Services Board. Her scholarship includes articles and scholarly presentations on social group work, mentoring, child welfare, divorce/separation and domestic violence. She is a member of the editorial board of the journal *Groupwork* and a reviewer for the journal *Community Mental Health*. Among the many groups that she has facilitated during a long social work career, one that stands out was a statewide task group she facilitated while working for the Arizona Supreme Court's Administrative Offices. Cheryl was the facilitator of a group consisting of community leaders, diverse professionals and lay people that worked together to pass a state law mandating that all divorcing parents in Arizona go through a psycho-educational group focused on their children's needs. She finds that social group work is a powerful social work intervention that can help people who are in pain and/or want to heal, grow, be productive and serve others.

The Contributors

Alana Atchinson, PhD, MSW, is a quintessential generalist social worker and has over 30 years of social work experience. She has worked in various fields including domestic violence, HIV/AIDS prevention and education research, child and adolescent mental health, rural poverty, and LGBT advocacy. In 2007 she joined the social work faculty at Bloomsburg University, Department of Social Work, in Bloomsburg, Pennsylvania, USA. She is an Associate Professor and teaches group work, introductory practice experience, and introduction to social work and social welfare. Alana Atchinson's email address is: aatchins@bloomu.edu

Michael J. Austin, PhD, MSPH, MSW is the Mack Professor of Nonprofit Management and Director of the Mack Center on Nonprofit and Public Sector Management in the Human Services, School of Social Welfare, University of California, Berkeley, California, USA. He is the former dean of the University of Pennsylvania, School of Social Work, He teaches non-profit management, community planning and the social environment dimensions of human behavior. He has many publications. Mike Austin's email address is: mjaustin@berkeley.edu

Robert Basso, PhD, is Associate Professor, Lyle S. Hallman Faculty of Social Work, Wilfrid Laurier University, Waterloo, Ontario, Canada. He is currently the Associate Dean of Laurier Brantford's new BSW Program. He has been a practicing social worker for almost four decades. He teaches group work and research. Robert Basso's email address is: rbasso@wlu.ca

Willa J. Casstevens, PhD, LCSW is Associate Professor, Department of Social Work, North Carolina State University, Raleigh, North Carolina, USA. She is a licensed clinical social worker. Dr. Casstevens worked in mental health in south Florida for approximately 15 years, and her research focuses on psycho-social and alternative treatment approaches and prevention. Her email address is: wjcasste@ncsu.edu

Michael George Chovanec, PhD, LICSW, is Associate Professor, St. Catherine University/ University of St. Thomas School of Social Work in St. Paul Minnesota, USA and has taught for the past 17 years. He has been a clinician for the past 35 years and works part-time as coordinator and group facilitator for a county domestic abuse program which he helped to develop in 1988. He is licensed as a Clinical Social Worker and Marriage and Family Therapist in Minnesota. His email is: mgchovanec@stkate.ed

Marcia B. Cohen, PhD, LCSW, is Professor, School of Social Work, University of New England, Portland, Maine, USA. She teaches courses in organizational change, social group work, and multilevel practice. Marcia also provides consultation to and serves on the board of several local agencies, is a member of the International Association for the Advancement of Social Work with Groups (IASWG), and is Co-Editor of the *Journal of Progressive Human Services.* Her email is: mcohen@une.edu

Mark Doel, PhD, MA (Oxon), CQSW, is Emeritus Professor, Centre for Health and Social Care Research, Sheffield Hallam University, Sheffield, England. He is a registered social worker and was in practice for almost 20 years. His research focuses on social work practice methods, especially groupwork. Mark is an active member of IASWG and was named an IASWG honoree at the Long Beach Symposium. His email address is: doel@waitrose.com

Alex Gitterman, EdD, MSW, is Zachs Professor and Director of the Doctoral Program, School of Social Work, University of Connecticut, West Hartford, Connecticut, USA. He is past president of the International Association for Social Work with Groups (IASWG) and has written extensively about life-model practice, vulnerable and resilient populations, and mutual aid groups. He was named an IASWG honoree at the Long Beach Symposium and also won the prestigious Lifetime Achievement Award of the Council of Social Work Education (CSWE) He can be reached by email at: Alex.Gitterman@uconn.edu

Ernest M. Gunderson, MSW (deceased), Minneapolis–St. Paul, Minnesota, USA had a 25 year engineering career prior to starting a second career in social work inspired by an interest in emotional healing. He obtained an MSW from St. Catherine University in 2011.

He had a passion for writing and also benefitted from Men's Support Groups, the subject of his *Proceedings* article.

Maria A. Gurrola, PhD, MSW, MA, is Associate Professor, School of Social Work, New Mexico State University, Las Cruces, New Mexico, USA. She teaches Human Behavior in the Social Environment. Her research interest is in transnational families and their resiliency while adapting to two different environments emphasizing mental health and gender issues.

Cheryl D. Lee, PhD, MSW, is Professor, School of Social Work, California State University, Long Beach, California, USA. See additional information in the section About the Editor. Her email address is cheryl.lee@csulb.edu

Kay Goler Levin, PhD, LCSW, is the Behaviorist in Advocate Lutheran General Hospital's Family Medicine Residency Program, in Park Ridge Illinois, and also serves as adjunct faculty in the School of Social Work and the Stritch School of Medicine of Loyola University Chicago. She leads Self-Hypnosis groups at Gilda's Club in Chicago and may be contacted at kglphd@gmail.com.

Lisa M. Murphy, PhD, MA, is an assistant professor of Criminal Justice at La Sierra University. She also has a teaching credential in Special Education. Her email address is: lmurphy0710@gmail.com

Barbara Muskat, PhD, RSW, is the Director of Social Work, the Hospital for Sick Children, Toronto, Ontario, Canada and an Assistant Professor (Status only) at the Factor Inwentash Faculty of Social Work, at the University of Toronto. Barbara is a member at large of IASWG's Board of Directors and former Chapter Chair of the Toronto Region's Groupworkers Network. Her email address is: barbara.muskat@sickkids.ca

William Pelech, PhD, MSW, is Associate Professor of Social Work at the University of Calgary in Calgary, Alberta Canada. His research interests include group work, social work education, FASD, child welfare and clinical practice. He has been the recipient of several major national research grants including a current grant which focuses on how practitioners harness diversity in service group development and therapeutic goals. He currently serves on the Board of the International

Association of Social Work with Groups and the editorial board of *Groupwork*.

Lorraine Ruggieri, LMSW, is a learning specialist and academic coach for students with learning disabilities in the Academic Access Program at Marymount Manhattan College located in New York City. She utilizes a holistic approach to AD/HD coaching and incorporates group work practice and a strength based perspective. She can be reached at lorraine.ruggieri@gmail.com.

Shirley R. Simon, ACSW, LCSW is Associate Professor, School of Social Work, Loyola University Chicago, Illinois, USA. She has been a social work educator for over thirty years, has published on group work education, practice and history, and has facilitated over one hundred student and alumni presentations at professional association conferences, particularly IASWG. Research and scholarship interests include group work education in MSW programs, hybrid-online group work instruction, curricular strategies for connecting students and professional associations, and social work dissertations on group work. She can be contacted at ssimon@luc.edu

Joanne Sulman, MSW, RSW, lives in Halifax, Nova Scotia and is a consultant in groupwork and qualitative research at Toronto's Mount Sinai Hospital and the University Health Network's Division of Thoracic Surgery. Her primary groupwork influence is the late Dr. Norma Lang. Joanne, an avid Groupwork Camper, is also an Adjunct Lecturer (status only) at the Factor-Inwentash Faculty of Social Work, University of Toronto, and a founding member of the Toronto Region Groupworkers Network. Her email address is: jsulman@mtsinai.on.ca

Edcil Wickham, MSW, is Professor Emeritus, Wilfrid Laurier University, Waterloo, Ontario, Canada. He is the first author of a book on group work practice with William Pelech and Robert Basso.

Introduction
and Editor's overview

Welcome to the exciting Long Beach International Association for Social Work with Groups (IASWG) Proceedings. The Proceedings include 11 articles that were submitted and accepted for publication by a team of reviewers and the editor. You, the readers, are in store for an amazing educational experience when reading these articles. They include key note addresses, papers and workshops that were presented June 2 - 5, 2011 at the 33rd Annual IASWG Symposium. The symposium brings together social group work scholars, practitioners and students from around the globe to share new ideas, experiences, theories, research and friendship. The participants are a diverse group of people who have in common a passion for social group work. These 11 articles are a representative sample of some of the fine work that occurred at the symposium. This year's theme "Social Group Work: We are all in the Same Boat" is weaved into each of the articles.

The Proceedings journey begins, as did the symposium, with the opening keynote address by Professor Emeritus, Mark Doel, from England. In article 1, he shares nautical metaphors about social group work with clever illustrations. The title, "All in the same boat - but where is the flotilla?" alludes to a serious aspect in this entertaining piece. He points out that many are not in the same boat.

As the symposium chair, I knew I had caught a big fish when I reeled in Alex Gitterman, the famous social work and group work scholar, to do a keynote address. It was amazing. The second article entitled: "Defining moments in groups: My personal journey," explains how Alex's thinking evolved as a group worker and group work scholar.

Mike Austin, a professor at University of California, Berkeley, School of Social Welfare and former Dean at the University of Pennsylvania, School of Social Work, gave the third keynote address. This lecture was sponsored by University of Southern California School of Social Work. Dr. Austin writes about task groups in social service/non-profit agencies and how to make these groups cutting edge learning experiences. He also expresses how group work has been a positive part of his career and personal life.

The next three articles relate to the intersection of social group work and higher education. Alana Atchinson, Lisa Murphy, Maria Gurrola,

Cheryl Lee, and Shirley Simon's article is about qualitative research on a telephone-mediated support group of social work professors of which they were members. Their article entitled "Academic mentoring of social work faculty: A group experience with a feminist influence" reports how a mentoring support group can be of great assistance to women social work professors on the tenure track in academia. Interestingly, most of these authors met each other for the first time in person at the symposium.

Lorraine Ruggieri, who works with college students who have disabilities, at Marymount Manhattan College in New York City, wrote an excellent article regarding college students with disabilities and the use of groups to support them. In her article entitled, "Balancing it all: A group initiative for students with learning disabilities who participate in the Academic Access Program", the group worker admits to mistakes which are good warnings for the reader.

Willa Casstevens and Marcia Cohen's article, "Using a reflecting team as a small group exercise in the social work classroom", will inspire you to create reflecting teams in your group work practice or in your social group work classroom.

Medical social group work comes to life in the next two articles, (7 and 8). Barbara Muskat and Joanne Sulman from Toronto, Canada, tell us everything we need to know about single session groups in a hospital in their superbly researched article, "How do we evaluate outcomes when the voyage is a single session?" This is a rarely written about topic. Kay Goler Levin's article, "Self-hypnosis groups for teaching relaxation and dealing with stress" is so interesting. Dr. Levin, is a seasoned group worker, and she explains how the group enhances self-hypnosis when used with cancer survivors.

Men's groups are the subject of the next two articles, 9 and 10. Ernest M. Gunderson, who died of Cancer, shortly after his manuscript was accepted for the Proceedings, did research on and was a longtime member of a men's support group in Minnesota, U.S.A. In his article, A Men's Support Group: An adjunct for Men in Psychotherapy", he explains that men often do not express as much emotion but often are just as depressed as women. He found that support groups can be very helpful to men. An excellent study on member engagement in interpersonal violence batterers' groups is the subject of the 10th article by Michael George Chovanec. He uses the Group Engagement Measure (GEM), an evidenced based instrument created by IASWG's Mark Macgowan, and his findings are very interesting. The last article,

"Harnessing the promise of diversity in group work practice", by Robert Basso, William Pellech, and Edcil Wickam from Canada is on a critical topic, diversity, in social group work. From interviewing different human service professionals, they develop their theory that diversity if properly addressed can enhance the group process and progress.

I hope that this overview has gotten you excited to read the Proceeding articles yourselves. Imagine yourself sitting in the beautiful Queen Mary state rooms, the dark paneled libraries with oval windows, or a deck chair overlooking the harbor. Then, take in the wisdom and knowledge of these fine authors who research, enjoy and find social group work practice useful for a variety of challenges diverse people experience.

Cheryl D. Lee
Editor

1

All in the same boat: But where is the flotilla?[1]

Mark Doel

Abstract:

flo•til•la (noun)
1. a fleet of usually small vessels
2. a group of things operating or moving together
Groups often characterize their members as 'all being in the same boat together' (Doel, 2006, p. 67). It is a nice metaphor and one that we can extend: can these individual groups see themselves as something larger, so that they become 'a group of things operating or moving together'? All in the same flotilla? In this plenary presentation I use my personal and professional experience as a groupworker and researcher to survey the potential for the group work fleet to set sail. I promise to extend the nautical metaphor pretty much to breaking point: choppy waters, unchartered courses, undercurrents and the doldrums are all likely to make an appearance.

Keywords: *Group work; groupwork; context; metaphor*

Introduction

Coming from an island nation I should be an ideal person to captain this particular plenary, splice the mainbrace and do all sorts of things like that, but in fact I am probably the world's worst seaman. I was sick on a crossing of the Mediterranean, the world's calmest sea. I was delighted when they opened the tunnel under the English channel and

---

1. This paper was given as the opening plenary to the symposium and it retains the conversational tone of its original delivery. It took place in the elegant surroundings of the Queen's Salon on *The Queen Mary*, Long Beach.

haven't been on a ferry since. So, though this confession provides no reassurance whatsoever about my ability to captain a ship, I can assure you that your metaphors will be in safe hands over this next hour.

Well, here we are all are, literally all in the same boat, *The Queen Mary*.

I wanted, first, just to say a few things about *The Queen Mary*. She was built in Clydeback, Scotland where, by a strange coincidence, not many months ago I led some groupwork training for social workers in the children's services. Or rather they led me, such was their experience and the breadth of their groupwork. *The Queen Mary* was the flagship of the Cunard White Star line. She held the Blue Riband for most of the years from her maiden voyage in 1936 through to 1952 – at that time averaging about 36mph for the transatlantic crossing. I feel a tingle to think that at the time I was born this vessel was *the* fastest way to cross the Atlantic by sea. She was converted to a troop ship during World War II (carrying Australian, New Zealand and US troops to the UK) and holds the world's record for most passengers ever carried at one time. In 1968 she was retired here to Long Beach, so she has had a long and rewarding retirement. As a new retiree myself, I am eager to get some tips from her.

Idioms

Idioms are notorious for losing their meaning when translated literally. For example, 'kicking the bucket' just means kicking a bucket in most other languages, but is a reference to dying in UK English. *We are all in the same boat* is an interesting idiom and, unlike many others, it does seem to translate into many other languages:

In French: *Nous sommes tous dans le même bateau.*
In Spanish: *Todos estamos en el mismo barco.*
In Italian: *Siamo tutti nella stessa barca.*
In German: *Wir sitzen im selben Boot* (actually, we *sit* in the same boat).
And in Hungarian: *We row in the same boat.*

But it is not entirely universal. The Serbs, for instance, are all in the same *sauce*; and, for the Cantonese, 'we are locusts in the same rope'.

Also: 'the cricket and the toad are inhabitants of the same shovelful of soil', which has some subtle differences from we're all in the same boat. I wondered about those desert cultures where I'm guessing boats do not play a very large part. So, in Arabic we are all the same in the wind (i.e., it will blow on all our faces with the same force).

Whatever the vessel or the medium, the notion that lies behind this idiom, *we're all in the same boat,* seems to be universal. It is telling us that *every-one is facing the same challenges and that we must help each other.* It figures in groupwork literature regularly – when it first appeared I do not know, but I think we can be sure that it was very early on and it fits so very well with our strong notions of mutual aid (Steinberg, 2009).

Naming groups

It is not hard to see why the boat is such a durable metaphor for a group. There is the obvious sense of rescue and intimacy, of combined purpose and mutual support. There are other parallels which I think are less self-evident. One of these is the process of *naming.* I am often intrigued as I walk past a marina and see all the boat names as to what brought the owners to their decision. There are the 'clever' ones, like Wake My Day and, often, they are given women's names like Gabriella because boats and ships are one of the few objects in the English language that have a gender – she.

So, in the spirit of this idea of naming – whether it is the group or the boat – I would like to tell the first of three brief stories.

Story #1. The naming story

This ship has its own rather amusing naming story. It is, of course, named after Queen Mary, the consort of King George V. Until the ship's launch the name she was to be given was kept a closely guarded secret. Legend has it that Cunard, the ship's owners, intended to name the ship *'Victoria'*, in keeping with company tradition of giving its ships names ending in "ia", but when company representatives asked the King's permission to name the ocean liner after 'Britain's greatest queen' (and they had the King's grandmother, Victoria, in mind) King George responded that his wife, Queen Mary, would be delighted! And so, the legend goes, the delegation had no other choice but to report that Hull No. 534 would be called *The Queen Mary* (Steele, 1995).

The naming of a group is a powerful act. As the creators of the group we often give the group a working title, like *The Tuesday Group* or *The Women's Group* to use in the planning stage. Too often this name sticks and *de facto* it becomes the group's name. However, this is a lost opportunity and, as good groupworkers, we know that a group gains a sense of its own identity when its members negotiate its own name with one another.

So, we are all in the same boat. Except, of course, we aren't!

We are not all in the same boat

Whether we are talking about a structural level or a personal one, we find there are very different kinds of 'boat'. The government in the UK pretends that 'we are all in the same boat' when it comes to the impact of the savage cuts in services that it has set in motion, but we know this not to be true. Some groups in society – poorer people, women, children – will be hit harder than others. There are some folks who are in such swanky boats they will barely notice the waves from these cuts ...

... And there are those who are so destitute that they can barely set sail in the first place. If they are in a boat at all, it is one that is not going to get them far. They will be devastated by the waves that the cuts to social services will make. They are most certainly in a different boat.

What is more, the swankier boats have been getting even swankier. In the UK the gap between the rich and the poor has steadily increased since the 1980s to levels last seen in the Victorian age.

There are some ways in which we might be 'in the same boat' but in very different situations and with very different opportunities. Here on this ship, *The Queen Mary*, for instance, there were three different classes of passenger: first class, cabin class and tourist class. Apparently, there were 711 in the first, 707 in the second (cabin) and

577 in the third (tourist) (Steele, 1995). Although they all departed and arrived at the same time and they were all equally dependent on the seaworthiness of the same boat for their safety, of course they had very different experiences of that journey.

As groupworkers we are in an interesting position. We are *in* the boat with the group members but we are not (not usually anyway) in the *same* boat in my metaphorical sense. Our life situations are likely to be different from the other members of the group. And yet we can and do call ourselves members of the group, too. It is this wonderful ambiguity that I find so attractive about groupwork.

Anyway, back to the boat. So, when we are told that we are all in the same boat when it is clear that we are not – and I am talking here about the bigger social picture – what is it time to do? It's time to start rocking the boat!

Story #2 The rogue wave story

Here is a literal story of a boat being rocked, in this case by a rogue wave. In December 1942, *The Queen Mary* was carrying 16,000 American troops from New York to Great Britain, a standing record for the most passengers ever transported on one vessel. While 700 miles from Scotland during a gale, she was suddenly hit broadside by a rogue wave that may have reached a height of 92 ft. Dr Norval Carter, part of the medical crew on board at the time, wrote that at one point *The Queen Mary* "damned near capsized... One moment the top deck was at its usual height and then, swoom! Down, over, and forward she would pitch." It was calculated later that the ship tilted 52 degrees, and would have capsized had she rolled another 3 degrees. Apparently, this incident inspired Paul Gallico to write his story, *The Poseidon Story*, which was later made into a film by the same name, using the *Queen Mary* as a stand-in for SS Poseidon.

Rocking the boat

As groupworkers we know that sometimes we need to rock our own boats; shake a group that is avoiding a taboo issue or where the process is stuck (Gitterman, 2005). This takes real courage because people do not appreciate their boat being rocked, not at the time. They will be scared, they will tell us we are not looking after them, they will say we are making them feel sick, and indeed we will wonder if we are abusing our authority. Above all, there *is* always the very real risk that we will rock the boat just that bit too much, that extra 3 degrees, and sink it! As groupworkers we are frequently in a position where we need to rock the bigger boat, the ship of state that is the Establishment. This liner is too often indifferent to the concerns of the people with whom we work, as social workers and groupworkers. This is a tough call. How do we rock the ship of state – it's very big! Physical force is not going to have much effect, so it requires 'smarts'. And I shall come back to this soon.

The sea

I have been reading a book recently about the development of language and the key place that colour has in this particular discourse (Deutscher, 2010). Although all societies have a word for the colour we recognise as red, there are a number of languages in the world that do not have a word for blue.

They describe blue as a variant of green or even use the same word as they use for 'dark' or 'black'. If you are part of a linguistic community that differentiates blue, is it possible to *see* blue if you do not have a word for it (that is the philosophical question); but also how can a society not discern blue when it covers half of their visual field, in the form of the sky; and even more if it is a sea-faring community? (That is the epistemological question).

Well, the sky and the sea are very easily taken for granted and this is rather a long way of saying that it is very easy to forget, when we use this idiom of all being in the same boat, that the boat is not without its context. This boat is *in the water*; or, at least, only of any use *when* it is in the water.

As groupworkers, it is natural for us to find that our main interests lie with what happens inside the group – in the confines of our boat. The group processes, the group dynamics, the skills of leadership and facilitation through sticky moments in the group, working with group taboos, with subgrouping and scapegoating, etc. I could go on – we all recognise the excitement and the challenge of developing mutual aid with a group of people over time. However, increasingly, we are appreciating the significance of *context* for successful groupwork. In our extended metaphor, we no longer take the sea for granted.

And so to my third story – nothing to do with the Queen Mary this time – but all to do with the 'sea' that our group/boats sail in.

Story #3: The scuttled story, or The group that was too successful

Jean and Kath were social work assistants in a large social work department in northern England. They attended a groupwork training course that brought qualified and pre-qualified social workers together for workshops and consultations over a six month period. Jean and Kath were in their thirties and they had had poor experiences of formal education; however, they lapped up the groupwork training and were very active participants in the workshops, loving this experience of adult learning. The course involved planning, recruiting, facilitating and – where appropriate – ending a group. Jean and Kath worked together in a day centre for people with learning disabilities and they started a group for eight of the women at the centre. It was a huge success for all the members. Just as one example, one of the women who had hitherto only communicated intermittently and then by swearing started to communicate more regularly and by drawing checks, crosses and sometimes pictures on the butchers paper (flip chart) that Jean and Kath supplied.

Jean and Kath were a success story, too. They blossomed, even physically, through the experience of leading the group and participating in the training. They attended one of the planned consultations even though they were both on leave from work at that time, and they were thrilled by the work they were doing and the positive effect it was having on the women.

Then, a few months into the work, they arrived at a consultation in very different spirits. Their manager had pulled the plug on the group. It was due to come to an end in a couple of weeks, but Jean and Kath had been planning to start another group. When the story was told, it was clear that Jean and Kath's success had caused resentment and jealousy in the wider staff group. Perhaps Jean and Kath could have been smarter, too – their enthusiasm had blinded them to the gathering storm. The group had obviously been seen as cliquish – a special room with 'Keep Out: group in progress' on the door, etc. So, though Jean and Kath had created a wonderful group with results for the members as good as you could wish for, they had failed to create a groupwork *service*. That group was just a one-off and their plans for an ongoing groupwork service were scuttled because they failed to pay attention to the wider context (Doel & Sawdon, 1999) – the 'sea' in which their boat was sailing.

So, where am I leading us?

Well, Jean and Kath were my groupworkers in the sense that I was co-leading the groupwork education programme that I referred to and I was co-supervising their practice. Once I had worked through the guilt at not having done a better job for them, I was able to reflect on the importance not just of the group but of *groups, plural;* that if more people are to benefit from what we all here know to be the power and healing of groups, then – of course – we need to join forces. It is ironic, because this is, after all, a basic groupwork principle.

The flotilla

So, we may all be in the same boat – all groupworkers committed to groups and groupwork – but shouldn't we coordinate our efforts to become a flotilla? At the very least, to avoid being scuttled like Jean and Kath; and more than that, to put into action the groupwork principles we know so well – that there is *strength in numbers* (Mullender & Ward, 1991). It is only by joining forces as a grand fleet that we can hope to have the kind of influence on the ship of state – the Establishment – that I mentioned earlier. We know from experiences in Germany after World War II, and I know personally from my experiences in post-soviet eastern Europe, what impact small groupwork can have on the larger society. But only if we join together.

So – we may all be in the same boat, but where *is* the flotilla?
And then I was reminded of the blue.

The blue

I was reminded of those societies without a word for blue, where the sea and the sky are a background, a context we can all too easily neglect to name.

I realised, of course:

We are the flotilla!

This great organisation, the International Association for Social Work with Groups (IASWG), which celebrates its third of a century at this Symposium, this is, *we are* the flotilla!

A veritable groupwork armada coordinating its full strength to mobilise against social injustice and inequality. All heading with serious intent in the same direction. So, whether you knew it or not, here we are in a rather interesting position – an armada inside a ship!

We each attend to and take care of our individual boats, sometimes even build them. We invite, coax and encourage people to climb in, to start to feel that they belong and then that they *own* this particular one. But it is vital that we make connections between these boats . . . these groups.

The first kind of connection is *recognition* – of the things that unite us – even if it is the differences that at first seem the most obvious. Then we need to get *organised* – join the local chapter of IASWG, for instance. We need to *test the waters* of our own experience by presenting papers and workshops, as many of you here will be doing over the course of the next few days, to see what our own experience of groupwork has to offer others, and what we can learn from them. Broadcast these experiences to help build practise, theory and the evidence base.

For these reasons, let me encourage you to go to sessions over the coming days at this Symposium that cover groupwork in fields with which you are *not* familiar, in order to throw new light on your own group context. Step into other people's boats.

Whatever you do, I hope and trust we will have a great symposium and, yes, I cannot resist a final nautical metaphor: let's push the boat out!

References

Deutscher, G. (2010). *Through the language glass: Why the world looks different in other languages.* London: Random House.

Doel, M. (2006) *Using Groupwork.* London: Routledge.

Doel, M., & Sawdon, C. (1999). *The Essential Groupworker.* London: Jessica Kingsley.

Gitterman, A. (2005). Group formation: Tasks, methods and skills. In A. Gitterman & L. Shulman (eds.), *Mutual aid groups, vulnerable and resilient populations, and the life cycle* (3rd ed., pp. 73-110). New York: Columbia University Press.

Mullender, A., & Ward, D. (1991). *Self-Directed Groupwork: Users take action for empowerment.* London: Whiting and Birch.

Steele, J. (1995). *Queen Mary.* London: Phaidon.

Steinberg, D. M. (2009). Mutual aid model. In A. Gitterman & R. Salmon (eds.), *Encyclopedia of social work with groups* (pp. 50-53). New York: Routledge.

2
Defining moments in groups: My personal journey

Alex Gitterman

Abstract: The paper focuses on my personal experiences as group member and leader/worker with special attention to defining moments in a group's life. From these experiences, I induct practice principles about group processes and practice interventions.

Keywords: defining moments, inductive, mutual aid, testing, group work practice and education

Introduction

Most practice-related scholarly talks and writings present at a conceptual level. In order to make the concepts accessible, some academics illustrate what the concepts look like in the real world of practice. For example, if we speak about depression theory and research, we identify the salient benchmarks associated with depression, including insufficient or excessive sleep, significant gaining or losing of weight, self-blame and punishment, and so on (Callahan & Turnbull, 2001; Smith, 2011). If a group member has these symptoms, the worker would, based on constructs and research, deduce that the member was depressed. In deductive reasoning, we begin with the concepts and look for connections in the real world. While deductive reasoning is the primary mode used for scholarship, I always have been equally interested and committed to inductive reasoning. With inductive reasoning, we begin with practice experiences and from their accumulation we develop generalizations in the form of practice constructs and principles. Induction is an equally disciplined and creative mode of thinking and reasoning.

Group workers need to reflect on two dynamics: (a) How much

our group members have taught us about group process and group intervention; (b) how much our observations and interventions were simultaneously affected by our knowledge as well as our instincts. With these two dynamics in mind, before I discuss defining moments in my professional group life, I would like to offer several observations about my experiences as a child and adolescent participant in groups. As a child, I grew up on the streets of the Bronx. All day, almost every day, my friends and I played some form of ball: stickball, punch ball, curb ball, stoop-ball, box ball, handball, basketball, football – just to name a few. And to break the routine up, we played Johnny on the pony, roller-skated, and missed lots of school. We spent more time with our peers than we did with our parents, as they were busy working and trying to make a living.

I observed firsthand the magnificence of peer support and peer camaraderie. I also saw, first hand, the destructiveness of being bullied, ostracized, and scapegoated. Unfortunately, I was both a contributor as well as a recipient of these behaviors. From these childhood experiences, I learned the profound impact peer groups have on one's sense of well-being and self-worth. I also learned the psychic damages that destructive peer forces can cause. I understood this on a visceral level, but not on a conceptual level until later, well into my adulthood, when I read the germinal work of Galinsky and Schopler (1977), *Warning: Groups May Be Dangerous.*

In my adolescent years, I learned the enormous value of supervised peer group activities, that is, the power of professionally led groups with a common purpose. The groups were the high school basketball and baseball teams which taught me the values of team work, watching each other's back, working through obstacles, and the euphoria of peer acceptance. I witnessed firsthand the "all in the same boat" phenomenon. Parenthetically, because of different peer experiences, my adolescence was blissful while my latency age was filled with turmoil.

In graduate school, as I studied linear stage theories of development that predicted the peacefulness of latency age and the turmoil of adolescence (Erikson, 1959, 1968; Sheehy, 1976), I became skeptical of these formulations as too often they did not apply to my life experiences. I inducted that the context of social class, ethnicity, race, gender, and immigration had a profound effect on life phases. Life was full of ebb and flow phases rather than linear stages (Germain, 1990).

With these introductory comments serving as context, I turn to professional experiences and defining moments in a group's life.

First-year internship

In my first year in field, I was placed in a settlement house and assigned two groups. The first was a teen group called the Impalas. I was their third group leader. I was unaware that this group had a ritual upon completion of the first meeting with a new social work student. When the meeting was over, I was asked to bang my hands on the table with the group members, and, on the count of three, all of us were to place our thumbs either in the upward position to signify that I did a good job in leading the group or in the downward position to indicate that I did not meet their standards. Well, on the count of three, as I looked up, all the group members' thumbs were in the downward position and only my thumbs were in the upward position. I was so shocked by the discrepancy of perceptions that I began to laugh uncontrollably.

In response, the members began to laugh uncontrollably at my shocked reaction and my uncontrollable laughter. When the laughter subsided, the members informed me that I was the first leader to pass their test as I did not crumble and that they valued a sense of humor. These members taught me a few invaluable practice lessons:

- In practice, be prepared to be tested.
- Do not personalize testing.
- The testing is not about you; it is about the differences in power.
- The testing is an opportunity to show your mantel, your professional competence.
- Do not take yourself too seriously.
- Humor is a social lubricant, a great bonder and powerful equalizer (Gitterman, 2003).

More than 50 years later, I am still grateful to these youngsters
I was also assigned to an after-school group for 11 year olds. Because of a prior summer camp experience with this age group, I approached the assignment with confidence. However, my confidence was short-lived. In graduate group work classes, I was learning various program skills and none of them were working. These youngsters were unmanageable. The more I structured prescribed activities and the more I reached for their feelings, the more they misbehaved. When I verbalized with a professional voice, "You seem to be having a bad day today," the youngsters would get wilder. The worker and group

members were locked into a cycle of mutual frustration. A youngster, Stevie, took matters in his own hands to end the status quo. As I passively asked the youngsters to stop knocking chairs over, Stevie came up to me and smacked me in my face.

At that moment, everything I was learning in graduate school left me, and I screamed, "You bunch of asses – that's it – no more of this shit – get your asses in your seats!" The youngsters ran to their seats, exclaiming, "Al is mad; oh, Al is mad." I apologized for my language, explaining that I was totally frustrated because they spend all their time knocking chairs over and running around rather than helping each other and having a good time together. I asked the youngsters what got in the way of their helping each other and doing things together. Stevie chimed in that the club leader was the major problem – "When you say something, it doesn't seem like you mean it." At that moment bells went off for me.

Stevie was telling me in words and action and telling the other members in action that I lacked congruence, that while I was frustrated and annoyed, my affect was totally bland. The youngsters were frightened by not knowing the depth of my anger and what I might do. Now, they saw me at my worst, using a few bad words, but with no abuse and no abandonment. At that moment the work began. I am indebted to Stevie and the group. Because of them, I have worked diligently to integrate my personal and professional selves, to integrate content and affect, and to strive for congruence. I also learned that the testing, disruptive group member is an ally rather than a threat. The "deviant" group member often speaks for the group and provides the group worker an opportunity to work on latent group issues. What wonderful teachers – I am grateful to Stevie and his buddies.

Youth Council

As a Youth Board gang worker, I reached out to existing gangs and transitioned them into social clubs. I also recruited neighborhood, natural groups into social clubs. The youth participated in wide-ranging activities from basketball tournaments to trips to raising money to purchase their club jackets. I formed an advisory Youth Council to which each group elected a representative. The Council was responsible for programs and policies and for dealing with disciplinary issues. The members had difficulty in one area – dealing with disciplinary problems. They had difficulty with assuming responsibility for disciplining their peers for problematic behaviors.

One particularly contentious area was drinking and fighting at Saturday night dances. When a member participated in such behaviors, she or he would have to appear before the Council for disposition. The Council members' responses were quite benign. As the dances became more problematic, members began to take on this responsibility more seriously. A defining moment came when the indigenous leader and president of the Council arrived intoxicated and disrupted a dance. The Council members had had enough. They showed individual courage and collective strength and voted to expel the president from the Council and suspended him for a month from the settlement house.

Unfortunately, I did not demonstrate a similar strength or courage. Fearing the loss of this youngster, I appealed for a more lenient punishment. At that moment, I lost the members' respect and the Council as a viable mechanism. I would like a "do-over" for this mistake. I learned that support had to be balanced with consistent demands; one without the other limits effectiveness. More than in my other roles, this experience taught the importance of integrating support and demand. While life rarely gives us opportunities for a "do-over," it does provide us with the opportunity to learn from our mistakes (as well as the mistakes of others) and to make new, more sophisticated mistakes. A powerful lesson!

My first teaching experience

The chair of the group work department, Professor Bill Schwartz, invited me to teach a group work course to non-majors. The class was composed of approximately 10 casework students, mostly female, and approximately 10 community organization students, mostly male, many of whom were former Peace Corp and Vista volunteers. Before long, I realized that these students were being socialized into two different professions.

The casework students were being socialized into the profession's treatment traditions. They had learned advanced engagement and exploratory skills; however, they were "blind" to social injustices and oppression. All problems were lodged in the person.

In contrast, the community organization students were being socialized in the profession's social reform tradition. They were impressive in their analyses of social injustices; however, they were relatively unskillful in interpersonal matters. When asked to role-play an interpersonal conflict between two leaders on a tenant's council, they mostly lectured, took sides, or withdrew and worsened the conflict.

Before my very own eyes, I found that half of the students were being trained to be metaphorically "blind" and the other half to be metaphorically "lame." For the clients, the choice between a metaphorically "blind" and "lame" worker is not a great choice. The only worse fate for a client is to be assigned to a social worker who is both metaphorically "blind" and "lame."

After a few classes, a conflict emerged between the casework and community organization students. The community organization students disparaged and intimidated the casework students.

The gender differences added to the problem. I tried to mediate the conflict. However, the abrasive behavior continued. When I set demands on the community organization students to be respectful in the class discussions, they responded quite creatively. They adapted a community organization strategy and went on a silence strike. Their silence was deafening and really threw me off stride.

Fortunately, I had recently read Bennis and Sheppard's (1956) classic article on stages of group development. I learned that challenges to a leader's authority were essential to the development of mutual aid. The article represented a career defining moment for a brand new teacher. It helped me not to define myself as a colossal failure and a totally inept teacher. Rather, it normalized and universalized the class experience; it helped me to focus on obstacles to peer learning. In the subsequent class, I thanked the community organization students for their silence, for taking the initiative to identify a significant class obstacle. They were thanked for letting me know the seriousness of the class obstacle, and for giving the class a chance to deal with it. I realized that class discussions were challenging basic assumptions about social work practice. The casework students were being challenged for their limited attention to the social context for their clients' troubles; the community organization students were being challenged by their limited attention to direct practice skills; and their teacher was being challenged by his uncertainty, as a new teacher, about how to help them learn from each other. Bennis and Sheppard (1956) helped me to reframe the silence strike from being a threat, to providing an opportunity to deal with the obstacles to peer learning.

After the community organization students shared their frustration, I reached for the frustrations of the casework students. The students began to listen to each other and to view the different professional strengths as providing opportunities for learning from each other rather than threatening each other. The work took off; the students took a major step toward becoming one profession.

This class had a profound effect on my selection of teaching to be both my avocation as well as my vocation. These students taught me that every class has the potential to be a learning group in which peers can learn from each other as well as from the teacher.

I also learned that heterogeneously composed class groups have sub-groups built in which create potential internal communication and relational obstacles; however, if they can be overcome, these class groups have the potential for intense impact.

Later in my career, I learned that the intensity of the felt need had a strong impact on overcoming these internal obstacles. The greater the felt need, the lesser the heterogeneity created relationship and communication obstacles (Gitterman, 2005). Most of all, I learned to allow the students and my clients to become my major teachers about both social work practice and about teaching social work practice.

Girls' adolescent group

On a sabbatical, I wanted the experience of working with a girls' adolescent group. I volunteered at a local high school. Eight girls signed up for a group to focus on every day issues in school, with their parents, friends, boys, etc. The guidance counselor introduced me to the girls as Dr. Gitterman. The girls were quite uncomfortable, viewing me as a "shrink." I was also very uncomfortable with the girls. Many of the girls were wearing mini, mini skirts and, in talking to them, I found myself looking at the ceiling. The conversations were stilted.

At the outset of the fourth session, one member, Jennie, broke the awkwardness by asking if I would be willing to share the happiest and saddest day of my life. I was immediately struck by the brilliance of the question. Jennie was testing my willingness to be more personal and intimate. If I had responded, "We were here to talk about you and not me," I would have lost the group.

After I answered that the birth of my children were the happiest days and the loss my father were the saddest days, the girls began to share the painful losses in their lives. That was all they needed, for the group worker to be more human. The work then took off in a most meaningful way.

As I reflected on this experience, I was struck by how the group members creatively knocked me off my professional pedestal and, simultaneously, had me become more intimate with them. This was one of my early inklings that female groups might deal with the authority theme somewhat differently than male groups.

At one point Professor Roselle Kurland asked me to review Linda Schiller's brilliant article (1996), "Stages of development in women's groups: A relational model." As the light bulbs went off, I immediately thought about this girls' group. Schiller (2007) and others (Kelly & Berman-Rossi, 1999) have expanded the formulation to other vulnerable groups.

Conclusion

In this paper, I attempt to demonstrate the interrelated uses of deductive and inductive reasoning to guide group work practice. The paper emphasizes my uses of accumulated practice experiences to induct group work practice principles. Practice insights are shared to encourage social workers to learn consistently from their practice. In reality, group work practice occurs at a dizzying speed with the worker (as well as the members) processing numerous messages and themes. The worker instantly has to decide which to reach for, which to table, and which to invite the group to determine. The worker's practice cannot be perfect; mistakes have to be made. The professional task is to reflect, to learn from one's mistakes, and to make newer, more sophisticated mistakes in the future. I hope that this paper encourages the readers to reflect and risk making more sophisticated mistakes.

References

Bennis W. G., & Sheppard H. A. (1956). A theory of group development. *Human Relations, 9,* 415-37.

Callahan, J., & Turnbull, J. E. (2001). Depression. In A. Gitterman (Ed.), *Handbook of social work practice with vulnerable and resilient populations* (pp. 163-204). New York: Columbia University Press.

Erikson, E. H. (1959). Identity and the life cycle. New York: International Universities Press.

Erikson, E. H. (1968). Identity, youth and crisis. New York: Norton.

Galinsky, M. J., & Schopler, J. H. (1977). Warning: Groups may be dangerous. *Social Work, 22*(2), 89-94.

Garland, J. A., Jones, H. E., & Kolodny, R. L. (1965). A model for stages of development in social work groups. In S. Bernstein (Ed.), *Explorations in group work: Essays in theory and practice* (pp. 251-294). Boston: Boston University School of Social Work.

Germain, C. B. (1990). Life forces and the anatomy of practice. *Smith College Studies in Social Work, 60*(March), 138-52.

Gitterman, A. (2003). The uses of humor in socil work practice. *Reflections, 9,* 79-84.

Gitterman, A. (2005). Group formation: Tasks, methods and skills, In A. Gitterman & L. Shulman (Eds.), *Mutual Aid Groups, Vulnerable and Resilient Populations, and the Life Cycle* (pp. 73-110). New York: Columbia University Press.

Kelly, T. B., & Berman-Rossi, T. (1999). Advancing stages of group development theory: The case of institutionalized older persons. *Social Work with Groups, 22*(2/3), 119-138.

Sheehy, G. (1976). *Passages: Predictable crises for adult life.* New York: F.P. Dutton.

Schiller, L. (1995). Stages of development in women's groups: A relational model. In R. Kurland & R. Salmon (Eds.), *Group work practice in a troubled society,* (pp. 117-138). New York: The Haworth Press.

Schiller, L. (1997). Rethinking stages of development in women's groups: Implications for practice. *Journal of Social Work with Groups, 20,* 3-19.

Schiller, L. (2007). Not for women only: Applying the relational model of group development with vulnerable populations. *Journal of Social Work with Groups, 30,* 11-26.

Smith, E. (2011). Mood conditions. In N. Heller & A. Gitterman (Eds.), *Mental health and social problems: A social work perspective* (pp. 331-335). New York: Routledge.

3
Groups as anchors in times of turbulence:
The centrality of group dynamics in transforming human service agencies into learning organizations[1]

Michael J. Austin

Abstract: *This keynote presentation gave me the opportunity to think more about the extensive role of groups in my teaching, research, consulting and self-care. It is divided into four parts and begins with some personal reflections on my experiences with groups. Secondly, I focus on group dynamics and some of the core concepts that I use in teaching my MSW students who are interested in management and planning. Thirdly, I want to share some highlights of my research related to building learning organizations inside human service agencies. And finally, I reflect on some promising group work practices.*

Keywords: *group dynamics, learning organizations, human services*

Personal reflections

My group work experience began decades ago with teens in both community programs and residential summer camp programs. Since those early days in my career as a social worker, I have spent time consulting with task groups, primarily in the area of strategic planning using a participatory model that involves the participants in shaping

1. This chapter is based on a keynote address at the 33rd Annual Symposium of the Association for the Advancement of Social Work with Groups (AASWG), Long Beach, CA., 2011.

their own future. One of my penultimate group work experiences as dean of a school of social work was trying to get everyone focused on the same topic, hopefully headed in the same direction, and equally committed to the implementation of organizational changes.

Over the past two decades I have been fortunate to have the opportunity to work with some very talented agency directors in both the public sector (county human service agencies) and the non-profit sector (family and children's services agencies) in the San Francisco Bay Area. Operating as members of think tanks and support groups, these agency directors have very few opportunities to share the challenges that they face in their daily practice (ranging from firing a senior manager to exploring the future directions of their organizations). I have served as the group facilitator for think tanks serving both the public sector and nonprofit sector groups.

While I have rarely identified myself as a group worker, I have spent my entire life doing task-oriented group work. My group work practice has also been informed by my hobby of a cappella choral singing that requires special listening in order to blend with other voices. In addition, my volunteer work in organizing the adult children of the residents of a retirement facility continuously reminds me of the group work skills needed to combine the needs for support group activity with action group activity.

Core group dynamics concepts

Over many years of teaching, I have sought to help students understand the processes of working with groups, whether they are agency boards, advisory committees, staff teams, interagency groups, or client advisory groups. As a facilitator of classroom discussions, it has become increasingly apparent to me that the nature of our student learning population has changed substantially. The under-30 population (The Millennials) has grown up digitally, with a new set of learning expectations related to customization, freedom to search, innovation, exploration, and opportunities to engage in social networking inside and outside of the classroom, that has caused me to totally rethink my classroom group work processes (i.e., the era of the "sage on the stage" is over).

While I see myself as a teacher of macro practice, I also teach theory for practice in our Human Behavior and Social Environment sequence, especially the use of theoretical concepts as tools for informing practice. In addition to thinking conceptually in order to assess a wide variety of group, community, and organizational dynamics, I also help students in my management and planning course to think strategically in order to collectively manage and guide change processes. To reach these goals, I often return to the pioneering group work of Kurt Lewin (1952) who encouraged us to move beyond the interpersonal dynamics in groups to focus on the external influences upon groups. He noted that "there is nothing more practical than a good theory"(p. 152) and I have modified that view to suggest that "there is nothing more practical than a set of concepts to inform the assessment and action phase of practice." This involves thinking both conceptually and strategically.

So when it comes to teaching about groups, I focus on the importance of clear goals, leadership, and the nature of organizational support needed by groups to promote learning and outcomes. In addition to identifying the structural and process aspects of groups (e.g., membership motivation, group cohesion, member roles), I emphasize the stages of group development (e.g., forming, norming, storming, performing, and adjourning) from the field of organizational psychology. I help students understand the importance of balancing group "tasks" with group "processes" as they emerge in many different types of groups (staff groups, boards, inter-agency task forces, etc.). I assume that most forms of group work seek to balance the interests of participants in taking action (task) with those more concerned with participation in shared problem-solving processes. Central to these dynamics are the communications concepts of sending, receiving, and trust-building.

Similarly, managing conflict and managing power are key concepts related to group leadership that can be understood as "informal" (anyone can lead from any position) to "formal" (where leadership is ascribed or achieved). I help students get in touch with decision making and problem solving frameworks that are relevant in providing leadership and creativity and are critical for managing the diversity of participants and ideas.

As noted in Figure 1, I have organized the considerable literature on group dynamics into a set of key constructs related to group structures (e.g., stages of group development, power and leadership, and diversity) and concepts related to group processes (e.g., conflict and change, systems of exchange including the role of self-interest, and integrating

Figure 1. Assessing the Dynamics of Groups Theory for Practice

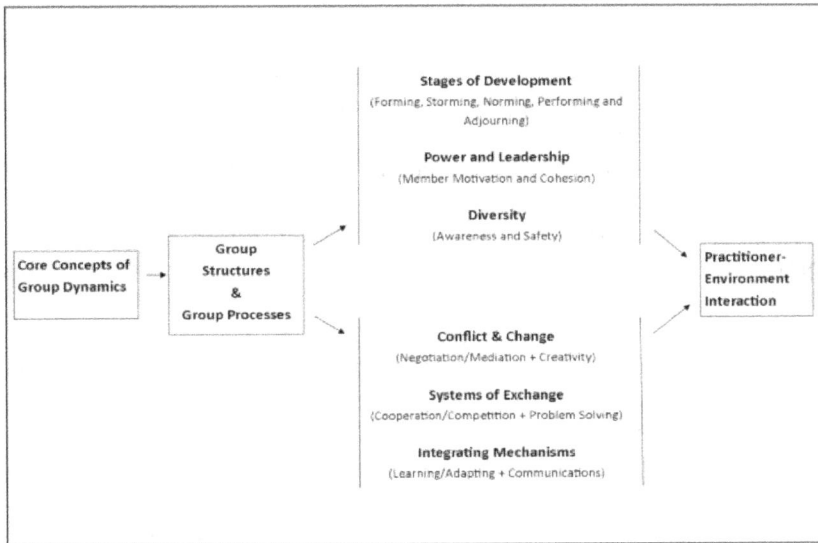

mechanisms that seek to capture staff, client, and community voice). In addition, I focus on practitioner-environment interaction to help students understand that their mere presence in a group can influence its structure, process, stage of development, diversity, power and leadership, conflict and change, systems of exchange and integrating mechanisms. For example, when fieldwork students are introduced to staff as interns in their agency staff meeting, their mere presence can impact the dynamics of the staff group.

Learning organizations

Over the past two decades, there has been a growing interest in identifying ways for organizations to become learning organizations. Garvin (1998) defines a learning organization as:

> an organization skilled at creating, acquiring, and transferring knowledge, and at modifying its behavior to reflect new knowledge and insights;" and

an organizational learning culture as "an environment that promotes and fosters individual, group, and organizational learning. (p.51)

For example, for schools of social work to become learning organizations (beyond the specialized interests of individual faculty), they need mechanisms to monitor the changing nature of practice in order to demonstrate their capacities as a learning organizations to be responsive to the profession as well as build a culture of sharing and learning inside the organization.

The key concepts relevant to the development of a learning organization were identified by Peter Senge (2006) in the early 1990s and these include:

- systems thinking -- seeing multiple relationships between people/ideas/things.
- personal mastery -- clarifying what's important
- mental models -- clarifying and adjusting underlying assumptions
- shared vision – capacity to articulate a future based on change
- team learning – using and sharing insights and learning

For example, an organization's strategic plan is designed to answer the question "where are we going?" All the elements of Senge's framework are involved in the development of a strategic plan.

So, if you walked into an organization that perceived of itself as a learning organization, what might you see? Garvin (1998) suggests that you would see many of the following processes reflected in daily practice:

- engaging in problem solving based on gathering information;
- engaging in experimentation;
- learning from promising practices; and
- learning from the past (see twelve organizational histories of pioneering human service agencies in the Bay Area) (Austin, 2013). From those serving children and families to those serving minority communities, these teaching cases provide my students with a longitudinal view of sustainability.

So the core group work task in a learning organization involves designing learning settings whether there are forums, staff meetings, off-sites, or audits. Secondly, promoting a culture of learning means valuing dissent in our agencies so that staff can feel safe to share provocative ideas and not share them outside the group where they can not be heard, respected and supported. Safe and open environments to share knowledge and practice wisdom are very much part of promoting a culture of learning.

Obviously an aspect of promoting a learning process is the group work activity of questioning, listening and responding. And finally, demonstrating a personal investment in learning is critical and helps me focus on the question of how to locate the research-minded practitioners working in our organizations. For example, if you were to think about any of your colleagues or supervisees and tried to identify those who might be research-minded practitioners, I am not sure how easy a task that it might be. It is not clear to me that a learning organization can succeed if there is no support or safety for staff who are coming to work every week wondering about the question: "Isn't there a more effective way to do this, or isn't there a more efficient way to do this?".

As I search for ways to identify or define the major elements of research-minded practitioners both in the US and in England, I have begun to identify three elements. One is clearly curiosity; namely, wondering if there is a better way to do what we are doing or a different way to do what we are doing. Curiosity can be related to one of our biggest challenges in human service organizations; namely, trying to define and measure our service outcomes. A second element relates to the process of engaging and reflecting on one's practice in the form of ongoing self-reflective practice. And the third characteristic of research-minded practice is critical thinking; namely, the ability to hear or read somebody's ideas and not "swallow them whole" but simply pause to think about what are some of the underlying issues in this particular area (Austin, Dal Santo,& Lee, 2012). One of the things I have noticed in my research that involves busy practitioners is the tendency to "swallow things whole" or to reject them out of hand (e.g., "that study was done in another part of the country or that's not the same kind of population as ours"). So the process of critically thinking about research or promising practices represents an important element in supporting research-minded practitioners seeking to promote the elements of a learning organization.

Search for promising group work practices

There are many different levels in our human service organizations where group work is taking place (e.g., executive director level, board level, staff teams, supervisory and program groups, peers inside and outside the agency, and client advisory committees in groups). Each of these levels is a venue for promising group work practices. Capturing the voice of staff and clients is critical for becoming a learning organization and human service agencies are making increased use of in-house surveys to gather staff opinion as well as periodic client satisfaction surveys to capture client voice.

One example of promising group work practices comes from my experience in developing a managerial leadership development training program for experienced clinicians who had moved into program management. When we asked the agency directors to identify the set of management skills that they thought should be incorporated into the structure of the training program, they identified classic management skills related to finance/fundraising, human resource management and information systems management (Austin, Regan, Samples, Schwartz, & Carnochan, 2011) . When we ask the program participants about their learning needs, they identified issues related to time management, dealing with senior management, dealing with the expectations of being a manager, managing conflict, and responding to changing client needs. Besides the different perceptions of learning needs from two different groups, we discovered considerable confusion about the role of a manager captured by the following metaphor: some who wore the manager's hat found it to be too small, others found that it was too big, and the third group found that the hat fit but when they looked in the mirror, they did not like the way they looked. As a result of the input from both groups, we became increasingly aware of the need to focus more attention on the identity and role of a manager before we could focus on the issues of leadership. These managers identified heavily with clients and the services that they were delivered and the resulting tension between their identities as social workers and their role as managers was both significant and unresolved (Austin, Regan, Gothard, Carnochan, 2013). The promising group work practice derived from this example relates to the co-construction of curriculum by involving the participants. The same practice will be used in the first few weeks of my management practice course when I seek to co-construct the course outline with the students. Another example of promising group work practice comes from my work in England and the role of local authority "link officers" in public social service agencies where a middle manager (e.g., training officer, research officer, program manager) is given an expanded job portfolio to link the external research environment with their service units by monitoring the dissemination of current research and sharing relevant studies or reports with the staff members engaged in work that relates to the studies (e.g., an article on group work with foster parents is shared with staff who have been struggling with that population and it becomes a topic for a staff meeting where the link officer facilitates the discussion and engages in follow-up).

Another area of promising group work practice relates to the process of bringing together clients or service users to share their views of their experiences as service recipients. I am particularly interested in what is happening in Scandinavia where they are bringing service users into the classrooms, not just to speak and tell them what it is like to be a service user, but actually admitting clients as co-learners directly into a university course with social work students and thereby promoting shared learning in a group environment that is instructor facilitated (Angelin, in press).

Another promising group work practice involves the substantial leadership transition taking place in many of our human service organizations with the retirement of the baby boom generation and the need to capture the knowledge of experienced staff before they leave the organization. With an immense amount of institutional memory walking out the door, there is often no system to capture the lessons learned from fighting bureaucratic battles, learning the tricks of the trade, and documenting effective workaround processes. For example, one agency videotaped an interview with a retiring 30-year chief financial officer in order to capture the tacit knowledge and practice wisdom that he had in his head that was not written down. This form of knowledge capture involved a group of staff with skills in the subject matter, interviewing, and the use of technology (Winship, 2012). Other examples of promising practices include

* Transforming staff training into staff learning events (co-constructed learning);
* Peer learning (journal clubs and online chat rooms);
* Client learning (service users groups);
* Surveys to capture staff and client voice;
* Engaging staff groups in data-mining (case record review);
* Educating new staff and board members;
* Creating think tanks as support groups.

Future questions to guide group work practice

While there are many questions that can be raised about the future of group work practice, I have selected a few. The first question relates to practice; namely, what are the best ways to incorporate groups of client and staff voices into learning organizations. We are affected by the case bias in our field of practice and need to balance it with a population orientation that we find in the field of public health in order to capture the voices of clients and staff.

Secondly, another group work research question relates to how we can foster our own inter-disciplinary practice and research in order to retain and expand the role the of group work in social work education. The challenge is to make the case and develop the evidence to support the centrality of group work competencies in all aspects of social work practice. What are the important elements of group work practice in the provision of casework services or in using group work within community organizing practices or facilitating groups in organizational or management contexts?

A third area of questions facing the future of group work relates to theory and our understanding of human behavior in the social environment in order to capture the reciprocal relationship between groups and the environment. How are the groups influencing environment and how does the environment influence groups? If one thinks about the future of group work in social work education from a marketing standpoint, we need to document the centrality of group work concepts buried in other approaches to practice in order to see how we improve the teaching of group dynamics in courses on human behavior and the social environment.

Conclusion

As I reflect on this journey today, I am struck by the special opportunity for me to assess the importance and centrality of group in all aspects of my professional practice. I am reminded of the importance of helping students and staff members *think conceptually* about the use of group dynamics concepts in order to inform all aspects of assessment (client, staff, organizational, communal, societal, etc) as well as the importance of *thinking strategically* about how we are managing organizations, improving communities, and changing public social policies. Obviously it is a challenge to bring group work back into the mainstream of social work education. I want to express my immense gratitude to all of you for giving me this time to share these ideas and hope these concepts will be useful in demonstrating the value of social group work practice in transforming human service organizations into learning organizations.

References

Angelin, A. (in press). Service User Integration Into Social Work Education: Lessons Learned From Nordic Participatory Action Projects. *Journal of Evidence-based Social Work*

Austin, M.J. (Ed) (2013). *Organizational histories of nonprofit human service organizations.* London: Routledge

Austin, M.J., Regan,K, Samples, M.,Schwartz, S. & Carnochan, S.(2011) Building Managerial and Organizational Capacity in Nonprofit Human Service Organizations through a Leadership Development Program. *Administration in Social Work* 35(3), 258-281

Austin, M.J., Dal Santo, T & Lee, C. (2012). Building Organizational Supports for Research- minded Practitioners. *Journal of Evidence-based Social Work.* 9(1/2), 174-2008.

Austin, M.J., Regan, K, Gothard, S.,& Carnochan, S (2013). Becoming a Manager in a Nonprofit Human Service Organization: Making the Transition from Specialist to Generalist. *Administration in Social Work* 37(4), 372–385.

Garvin, D. (1998). Building a learning organization. In Harvard Business Review (Ed).Knowledge management (pp.47-80). Boston, MA: Harvard Business School Press.

Gothard, S. & Austin, M.J. (2013). Leadership Succession Planning: Implications for Nonprofit Human Service Organizations.*Administration in Social Work,* 37(2). 272-281

Lewin, K. (1952). Field theory in social science: Selected theoretical papers by Kurt Lewin. London: Tavistock

Senge, P. (2006). *The fifth discipline: The art and practice of the learning organization*, New York: Doubleday.

Winship, K. (2012). Knowledge capture and the retirement of the director of finance: Succession planning in the San Mateo County Human Services Agency. Journal of Evidence-based Social Work. 9(1/2), 100-109

Senge, P. (2006). *The fifth discipline: The art and practice of the learning organization*, New York: Doubleday.

4

Academic mentoring of social work faculty:

A group experience with a feminist influence

**Alana B. Atchinson, Lisa M. Murphy,
Maria A. Gurrola, Cheryl D. Lee,
and Shirley R. Simon**

Abstract: *Using theory and principles of group process, and influenced by feminist theory of co-mentoring, a group of social work educators met monthly in a telephone mediated support group. The purpose of the group was to offer support to faculty involved in the tenure process in the areas of teaching, scholarship, and service. This paper offers an analysis of this experience. Suggestions for improved mentoring of social work faculty will be explored and areas for further research will be identified.*

Keywords: *mentoring, telephone mediated groups, social work faculty*

Introduction

The start of a new tenure-track faculty member's career can be a stressful time filled with job insecurities and questions about expectations. As the number of tenure-track faculty appointments has declined and new hires are held to increasingly higher standards of productivity, the sense of vulnerability on the part of new faculty has intensified (Finkelstein, 2003; Graubard, 2001). Mentoring can help new faculty succeed in academic life. The mentor-protégé relationship has been a subject of discussion and research in both the business and academic worlds for many years. Although the mentoring relationship may be an especially important tool for academic success for new social work faculty, discipline specific research exploring mentoring of junior faculty has been scant. This lack is evidenced not only in research journals but also in primary professional publications. For example, there was no entry for "mentor" in either the *Social Work Dictionary*, 3rd edition (1995), or the *Encyclopedia of Social Work*, 19th edition (1995). A more recent entry in the *Encyclopedia of Social Work with Groups* addresses mentoring but is not specifically about junior faculty in an academic environment (Lee & Montiel, 2009). Additionally, the few studies that specifically explore mentoring of *new* social work faculty focus exclusively on individual mentoring relationships (Wilson, Pereira, & Valentine, 2002).

Using theory and principles of group process, and influenced by feminist theory of co-mentoring (McGuire & Reger, 2003), a group of social work educators, four untenured and two tenured, met monthly, via telephone conference calls, to support the work of individual members and the group as a whole. This paper offers an analysis of this experience. Suggestions for improved mentoring of social work faculty are explored, and areas for further research are identified.

Review of literature

Women in academics

The field of academia has changed over recent decades as the number of women taking tenure track positions in universities grows; however, despite the increased presence of women on campuses, a disproportionate number of men continue to hold the majority of both high ranking administrative and full-time tenure track positions (Bakian & Sullivan, 2010). While men are more likely to hold full-time positions in research, women are commonly found as part-time faculty focused on teaching (Hart, 2011; Carr, 2001). This division is especially troublesome, as statistics show that in the last decade similar number of PhDs were awarded to men and women (Cantor, 2010). It is important to note that while the total number of PhDs awarded was split nearly evenly between men and women, when examining the individual numbers by field, gender division reflected a gross imbalance. Fields such as nursing and the humanities were dominated by women, while mathematics and sciences were heavily laden with males (Carr, 2001). Additionally, within this context, women experience advancement of research careers to a lesser degree than their male counterparts (Gardiner, Tiggemann, Kearns, & Marshall, 2007).

Mentoring

Research has shown that the mentoring process is essential for new professors to successfully navigate the world of academia (Gee & Norton, 2009; Wasserstein, Quistberg & Shea, 2007). This is particularly true for women, and examining gender bifurcation within the mentoring dyad has shown that within academia, the total number of male mentors outnumber female mentors, but those female mentors often had many more female than male protégés (Perna, Lerner & Yura, 1995). After a woman is hired in a tenure track position, the experience can be isolating, as demonstrated in an auto-ethnographic study by Hellsten, Martin, McIntyre, and Kinzel (2011), and women frequently experience the tenure track very differently from their male counterparts. In addition to isolation, women in the academy have reported discrimination and a social network that they are unable to access as two marked difficulties faced when navigating the world of academia (Foster et al., 2000; Wolfinger, Mason, Goulden, 2008). In 1999, Australia adopted an action plan to target inequalities in Australian universities, through which formal mentoring was used, under the assumption that when mentoring is informal, women may often be excluded (Gardiner, Tiggemann, Kearns, & Marshall, 2007). It seems universal that mentoring plays a positive role in improving the status of women in academia, and is shown to be most effective when there is a complementary fit between the mentor and the protégé, especially when the mentor is formally recognized and/or rewarded for his or her efforts in the process (Gee & Norton, 2009). Gee and Norton (2009) also observed that women should be cautious of time commitments outside of specific field work, as committee work can be time consuming and ultimately less advantageous in career advancement. Of course, it is also imperative for a successful mentoring relationship that a hierarchal system of oppression is not in place; to avoid that, some institutions favor peer mentoring as a means to connect similarly aligned faculty to reduce insecurities, which ultimately leads to further isolation (Driscoll, Parkes, Tilley-Lubbs, Brill & Pitts Bannister, 2009).

Family and social obligations

Family seems to be another area where, in the context of success in academia, women face more difficulties than male colleagues. This is particularly true for women who have children under the age of six (Wolfinger, Manson & Goulden, 2008). In fact, even when programs and services have been created to assist women with families, they are often reluctant to use these services through fear of appearing to be taking advantage of their position or being viewed as doing less work than women with no children or their male counterparts, regardless of the males' parental status (Hellsten, Martin, McIntyre & Kinzel, 2011). Wolfinger, Manson and Goulden (2008) also found that having a family has a different effect based on gender. For men, having a family, including children, has a positive effect; yet for women, the opposite was found. The same study also found that for single Ph.D. graduates, gender was not strongly indicative of their future success in academia; in fact, single women fared slightly better than men (Wolfinger, Manson & Goulden, 2008). Additionally, women often finish Ph.D. degrees during what is often viewed as prime childbearing years. This often creates a predicament for women who may be forced to choose between a family and a career (Mavriplis et al., 2010).

Mentoring social work faculty

New social work educators have reported that mentoring was especially beneficial to their teaching and research (Wilson, Pereira & Valentine, 2002). This qualitative study also found that new female social work educators valued the mentoring they received, especially with regard to networking and research (2002). It is important to note that even in the field of social work, a profession where women are the majority, high end administrative positions are still largely filled by men (Bent-Goodley & Sarnoff, 2008; Sakamoto, Anastas, McPhail & Colarossi, 2008). Social work as a discipline and practice strives for social justice, and the lack of women in administrative positions is an ongoing issue that is currently being confronted in this profession (Bent-Goodley & Sarnoff, 2008). In conjunction with social justice themes, knowledge about mentoring in social work education within underrepresented minority groups is not readily available; however, Simon, Perry and Roff (2008) found that a group of African American women sought and received more mentoring regarding their doctoral studies and faculty expectations than regarding balancing their career and family issues. The limited research on mentoring across cultural, racial, and gender barriers often addresses new models of mentoring, including new conceptualizations of roles, implementing practices that promote mentoring within academia, and the relatively new concept of multiple mentoring (Sorcinelli & Yun, 2007). For multiple mentoring, the mentoring process is a group- or partner-based journey, typically non-hierarchical, collaborative, and designed to mentor specific subject areas (Sorcinelli & Yun, 2007). In a study of gender differentiation among social work faculty at both Canadian and United States universities, Sakamoto et al. (2008) found that similarities exist between the two countries in regard to gender disparities. While there are far too many variables to make concrete assertions, similar patterns of underrepresentation emerge in terms of tenure, administrative positions, and promotions of female faculty members in both countries (Sakamoto et al., 2008).

Trust and mentoring in academia

Trust is a very significant factor that emerges in the literature regarding mentoring, and it is especially vital in those mentoring relationships that bridge gender and culture. It is easy to establish and perceive trust when both mentor and protégé have commonalities; yet, when differences exist, discomfort may arise, which if not properly navigated may develop into distrust (Shollen, Bland, Taylor, Weber-Main & Mulcahy, 2008). Shollen et al. also observed that trust leads to mutual understanding and symbiosis, and provides a space for growth and learning within the mentoring dyad (2008). Trust within academia is often difficult to achieve due to the constant competition for resources and promotions (Hart, 2011). Due in part to these reasons, trust is often avoided in order to reduce the vulnerability of women within academia. Often, non-spoken rules dictate actions that create a hostile environment, even when there is no clear threat to these women (Cantor, 2010). Research is vital to upward mobility in academia, and trust and expertise can have a negative effect on the mentoring relationship if both the mentor and protégé have a vested interest in the same area of research. In a study of female social work faculty, a new educator shared an area of interest in research with her mentor, and found that the mentor assumed a patronizing role, rather than offering expertise and respect as a colleague to the new faculty member (Wilson, Pereira, & Valentine, 2002).

Methodology

Design, data collection and analysis

The mentoring group met by phone for one hour once a month for a two year period. After meeting for 18 months, the group participants anonymously answered 10 open-ended questions (Appendix A) after receiving University Institutional Review Board approval. The results for each question were compiled and analyzed for themes in the responses. Two members of the group (not the group organizer) independently analyzed the responses. Inter-rater reliability was at an 85% level.

Sample

In this group of six, all of the members were female and ranged in age from 32-62. Three of the group members were white, two were Mexican-American, and one group member was Native American/White. Group members varied in academic rank. Four group members were untenured assistant professors. Among this group of untenured assistant professors, one each had finished her second, third, fourth, and fifth year. A fifth group member was a tenured assistant professor. The sixth group member was a tenured full professor. One of the group members was at a research one institution, three group members were at research two institutions and two group members were at primarily teaching institutions.

Results

The main overarching theme that came up during several questions was "trust." This theme was interesting for several reasons. First, most of the group members had never met one another in person. It is often difficult to trust people one has never met in person. Trust can be particularly difficult when one cannot see and observe the body language of the other group members during meetings. Also, the field of academia, like many other professions, is very small, and one is not always aware of the external relationships group members may have and how those relationships might influence one's future. Third, the different academic ranks of some of the participants created issues of trust and feelings of vulnerability. Lastly, because of trust and vulnerability at their home institutions, several group members had problems trusting the group in the beginning. For example, one group participant stated, "When I started with the group, I was hesitant to share issues that I felt vulnerable about. Over time I have come to trust the other group members and tend to trust more and share more."

Most of the group participants had experienced some form of mentoring at various points in their career. Many had experienced dissertation mentoring. Some participants had experienced mentoring at their home institution, while others had not. One group member said, "I work with a group of colleagues where the senior researcher serves as a mentor. She is guiding the group to projects and gets us involved in different projects to increase our research, publications and be successful in the tenure process." This was one example of a supportive mentoring environment. However, there were many examples of non-supportive home institution environments. One participant said, "I have looked for mentoring in my home institution but have not been particularly successful." A few of the group participants who had not experienced mentoring at their home institution had sought mentoring through professional organizations. For example, one group member said, "Prior to this experience I had approached mentoring through the Division on Women and Crime. There are several feminist scholars who are part of the Division that have been great resources."

Participants were motivated to join the mentoring group for several different reasons. A few group members were having trust issues at their home institutions and were looking for support during the tenure and promotion process. One participant explained her situation and her decision to join the group:

I met the group organizer at the group camp/group conference in 2008. After several conversations about academic life and the importance of mentoring, she invited me to join the group. Having been unsuccessful finding a mentor in my home institution, I was excited to join this group. I am nervous about the tenure and promotion process at my institution and was looking for support and input from other faculty. After a very difficult first year at my home institution, I was very hesitant to talk with colleagues because I did not trust them to not use information I shared against me during the evaluation process. I particularly like being able to talk with faculty from other institutions because of the trust issues I have at home.

A second reason members were motivated to join the group was to get support and feedback from others. One group member said,

It seemed like a good opportunity to learn more about the experiences of others and get support/feedback on issues that emerge regarding teaching and publishing from the point of view of someone outside of one's institution.

The convenience of the group was another reason members chose to join. Since the group did not require a large time commitment on the part of the group members and the meetings were via telephone once a month, members believed it was something they could fit into their schedules. One member said,

I also decided to join because I knew it was going to be by phone, this is convenient because I do not have to go out of my house and I can do it while I am cooking dinner or getting ready to put my kids to bed. Time is very limited when you have young children, and there is no time to go out of the home to meet with others and talk about what is going on in our job. This also gave us the opportunity to talk to people in other universities.

Lastly, some group members thought by joining the group they might be able to help other group members. One group member explained

I joined the mentoring group to help some of my colleagues. I believe in mentoring and wanted to give something which I wish I would have had.

Group members were asked if they thought mentoring in the group was different from individual mentoring. A few participants stated they did not notice any differences between individual and group mentoring. However, several group members listed some of the advantages and disadvantages they thought were present with this style of group mentoring. One participant thought an advantage of group mentoring was that it involved a "more collaborative process with equality among peers." Another participant said, "Mentoring in a group is nice because I like when other people bring up issues that I have been thinking about. It makes me feel like I am not alone in my experiences or how I am feeling." However, mentoring group participants did believe there were a couple of disadvantages. One participant believed there was "less time to focus on one's personal issues." Another participant stated, "At least in my case, I do not personally know all of the group members so this may play a role in how much I'm willing to share about specific issues." The disadvantages listed by participants were considerably fewer than the advantages listed. Overall, group members saw much benefit to the group mentoring process.

Participants were asked what they would change about the group. Group members suggested they wanted to work on building the trust in the group. One group member explained,

I am little more cautious about some of the issues I raise in the group setting. I have had some very bad experiences and don't always have confidence that people will keep things within a group. When I was going through some of the stuff with my former employer I didn't say everything that was going on. However, I did share some of it. This group was nice because they listened and kept stuff in the group. As I was seeking mentoring in my former department, I attempted individual mentoring and those people were not trustworthy so I guess it just depends on the group and the individual person and you always need to be aware of who you can trust and who you can't.

Two of the group members work in the same department at the same institution, which also led to some hesitancy about which subjects might be discussed in the group, especially because one member had a higher rank than the other group member. There seemed to be a fear among group members that what was said in the group might not stay in the group.

The meeting time was another thing some members wanted to change. However, there was some discrepancy among group members about the time of day that worked the best. For example, one group member stated, "The time is difficult for me. I am the only member on the East Coast so the calls are late for me. However, I find the benefits of being a part of the group to outweigh this inconvenience." On the other hand, one group member suggested, "It would be nice to have conversations a little later in the evening so I can participate a little more." The mentoring phone calls usually took place around five o'clock in the evening Pacific Coast time. A few group members wanted to change the structure of the meetings. One suggestion was to initiate a better method of communication (i.e., video chat or other online processes)." The role of the group participants was another issue that was suggested as a way to improve closeness and trust in the group. One participant observed, "Our current project is this research. It's brought us closer together I think so maybe more projects. Not sure of that since we are all so incredibly busy." These were all minor suggestions to improve the group overall but they appear to pertain to building trust and better group cohesion in the future.

Last, group members were asked how they thought diversity was dealt with within the mentoring group. Some group members reported that diversity was not addressed in the group while others thought it was adequately addressed. For example, one group member considered diversity to be a difficult issue for people to address so it was not dealt with at all, even though group members were very diverse. She stated, "We are diverse in many ways and we talk about it yet I don't think we touch on every issue of diversity. I think even in this setting it is difficult to talk about some issues." Yet, another group member found that there was an acceptance of the roles of others. She said, "One of the biggest differences is the parents and non-parents. Group members seem to be accepting of these differences. I feel the group members are open- minded about differences in culture. We could discuss this more." There seems to be room to discuss diversity in all of its different forms that affect women in academia, including the issues of parenthood and the decision to have or not to have children as an academic.

Overall, there are advantages and disadvantages to mentoring over the telephone but members seemed to enjoy the process and have benefitted from the group. One member stated, "When I started with the group, I was hesitant to share issues that I felt vulnerable about. Over time I have come to trust the other group members and tend to trust more and share more." Another participant shared, "I see how the group members help when individuals are down and out. This gives me a very positive feeling like the group is worth it. I've received a lot of support." These results support a feminist model of group mentoring that seems to have benefitted several junior faculty members as they navigate the tenure and promotion process. One group member summed up the group mentoring experience in the following way:

> *Rather than seeking guidance with help related to the specific process at my home institution, I tend to turn to the group for three things:*
> *1. As a place to discuss issues related to teaching*
> *2. As a place to find support and encouragement for scholarship*
> *3. For general camaraderie with other academics, ones I have grown to trust.*

Limitations

The study had a small sample size and may not be generalizable to other female social work faculty. Members of the group analyzed the data, which may have biased the results. Qualitative data by its nature has a subjective element.

Summary and recommendations

It was apparent in this qualitative study that mentoring of newer social work female faculty is desirable to improve success in the academic arena, which is consistent with prior research (Bent-Goodley & Sarnoff, 2008; Sakamoto et al., 2008; Wilson et al., 2007). Like other studies of mentoring in academia, this study found that mentoring is essential for traversing the tenure track process (Gee & Norton, 2009; Wasserstein, Quistberg & Shea, 2007). Members of the mentoring group who consisted of social work faculty found the group to be a place to discuss teaching and scholarship issues and to find friends to prevent isolation (Hellsten et al., 2011). Further, members received tenure, retention and/or promotions during the two year period of the group. Group mentoring, as opposed to individual one-on-one mentoring, allowed the members to discover that their issues were experienced by others and to garner mutual aid (Gitterman & Shulman, 2005). The use of telephone technology made the group accessible, especially for female faculty who also had young families. The literature discusses discrimination toward women with young children in academia who are often viewed as not doing their fair share of the work (Wolfinger et al., 2008; Hellstein et al., 2011). In contrast, the women who were parents of young children in this study felt they received support from other group members, including those who did not have young children.

As in other mentoring studies, trust was a major theme and is essential for mentoring to progress (Shollen et al., 2008). There were several factors that inhibited trust from developing in this group: most members had not met each other in person and feared that information would not be kept confidential within the relatively small social work academic community. In addition, the academic work place, which is highly competitive for resources, is known as a barrier to trust among faculty in general (Cantor, 2011; Hart, 2011). The results indicated that over time, the group became a safe place where members felt they could be more open and receive support even though members expressed past experiences in academia where trust was not found in individual one-on-one mentoring relationships.

Several recommendations emanate from this study. The results indicate that although mentoring in a group has some drawbacks such as less time to attend to an individual problem and a greater possibility of a breach in confidentiality, the members overall were satisfied with the group experience, felt they learned more from peer input than would be possible in one-to-one mentoring, and liked the convenience of meeting monthly by telephone. The implementation of additional mentoring groups are recommended but will require additional research since very few group mentoring studies have been completed.

The establishment of a mentoring group of members from varied institutions should be considered due to the competitive nature in most home institutions. Meeting by telephone was considered a plus but did preclude the reading of body language. The use of video technology is recommended to improve communication. The group decided to evaluate their mentoring experience, and this project brought the group closer together as they planned the research, wrote a manuscript, analyzed the data, and created a proposal and presentation for the IASWG international symposium. The group participants highly recommend group projects for this type of group. The fact that this mentoring group could meet in person at the IASWG Long Beach

Symposium was a special way to foster cohesion. A combination of technology mediated sessions with at least one face-to-face meeting at some point in person is highly recommendation.

References

Bakian, A. V., & Sullivan, K. A. (2010). The effectiveness of institutional intervention on minimizing the demographic inertia and improving the representation of women faculty in higher education. *International Journal of Gender, Science and Technology, 2*(2), 206-234.

Bent-Goodley, T.B., & Sarnoff, S.K. (2008). The role and status of women in social work education: Past and future considerations. *Journal of Social Work Education, 44*(1), 1-8.

Cantor, N. (2010). Women in the academy: Reflections on best practices for survival and success. *Office of the Chancellor.* Paper 2.

Carr, F. (2001). The gender gap in the academic labor crisis. *The Minnesota Review, Number 52-54 (New Series),* 271-279.

Driscoll, L. G., Parkes, K. A., Tilley-Lubbs, G. A., Brill, J. M., & Pitts Bannister, V. R. (2009). Navigating the lonely sea: Peer mentoring and collaboration among aspiring women scholars. *Mentoring & Tutoring: Partnership in Learning, 17*(1), 5-21.

Finkelstein, M. J. (2003). The morphing of the professoriate. *Liberal Education, 89*(4), 6–15.

Foster, S.W., McMurray, J.E., Linzer, M., Leavitt, J.W., Rosenberg, M., & Carnes, M. (2000). Results of a gender-climate and work-environment survey at a midwestern academic health center. *Academic Medicine, 75,* 653-660.

Gardiner, M., Tiggemann, M., Kearns, H., & Marshall, K. (2007). Show me the money! An empirical analysis of mentoring outcomes for women in academia. *Higher Education Research & Development, 26*(4), 425-442.

Gee, M. V., & Norton, S. M. (2009). Improving the status of women in the academy. *Thought & Action: The NEA Higher Education Journal,* 163-170.

Graubard, S. R. (2001). *The American academic profession.* New Brunswick, NJ: Transaction.

Gitterman, A. & Shulman, L. (Eds., 2005). *Mutual aid Groups, vulnerable and resilient populations, and the life cycle (Third Edition).* New York: Columbia University Press.

Hart, J. (2011). Non-tenure track women faculty: Opening the door. *Journal of the Professoriate, 4*(1), 96-124.

Hellsten, L. M., Martin, S. L., McIntyre, L. J., & Kinzel, A. L. (2011). Women on the academic tenure track: An auto-ethnographic inquiry. *International Journal for Cross-Disciplinary Subjects in Education, 2*(1), 271-275.

Lee, C. D. & Montiel, E. (2009). Mentoring. In A. Gitterman & R. Salmon, Eds., *Encyclopedia of social work with groups*, 306-308. New York, NY: Routledge.

Mavriplis, C., Heller, R., Beil, C., Dam, K., Yassinskaya, N., Shaw, M., & Sorensen, C. (2010). Mind the gap: Women in stem career breaks. *Journal of Technology Management & Innovation, 5*(1).

McGuire, G. M., & Reger, J. (2003). Feminist co-mentoring: A model for academic professional development. *Feminist Formations, 15*(1), 54-72.

Perna, F. M., Lerner, B. M., & Yura, M. T. (1995). Mentoring and career development among university faculty. *Journal of Education, 177*(2), 31-45.

Sakamoto, I., Anastas, J. W., McPhail, B. A., & Colarossi, L. G. (2008). Status of women in social work education. *Journal of Social Work Education, 44*(1), 37-62.

Seritan, A. L., Bhangoo, R., Garma, S., DuBe', J., Park, J. H., & Hales, R. (2007). Society for women in academic psychiatry: A peer mentoring approach. *Academic Psychiatry, 31*(5), 363-366.

Shollen, S. L., Bland, C. J., Taylor, A. L., Weber-Main, A. M., & Mulcahy, P. A. (2008). Establishing effective mentoring relationships for faculty, especially across gender and ethnicity. *American Academic.4*, 131-158.

Simon, C.E., Perry, A.R., & Roff, L.L. (2008). Psychosocial and career mentoring: Female African American social work education administrators' experiences. *Journal of Social Work Education, 44*(1), 9-22.

Sorcinelli, M. D., & Yun, J. (2007). From mentor to mentoring networks: Mentoring in the new academy. *Change: the Magazine of Higher Learning*, 58-61.

Wasserstein, A. G., Quistberg, D. A., & Shea, J. A. (2007). Mentoring at the University of Pennsylvania: Results of a faculty study. *Society of General Internal Medicine, 22*, 210-214.

Wilson, P., Pereira, A., & Valentine, D. (2002). Perceptions of new social work faculty about mentoring experiences. *Journal of Social Work Education, 38*(2), 317-333.

Wolfinger, N. H., Mason, M. A., & Goulden, M. (2008). Problems in the pipeline: Gender, marriage, and fertility in the ivory tower. *Journal of Higher Education, 79*(4), 388-405.

Appendix A. Qualitative questionnaire

- What other ways have you approached faculty mentoring prior to this experience?
- Tell me about your decision/motivation to join the mentoring group?
- How is mentoring in a group different from individual mentoring for you?
- What are the differences between issues you raise in a group setting and those you raise in individual mentoring sessions?
- How has the group changed over time for you?
- What have you taken from the group mentoring experience?
- How can we improve the group mentoring experience?
- What are the advantages and disadvantages of mentoring over the telephone?
- What are other comments you have about the mentoring group?

5
Balancing it all:
A group initiative for college students with learning disabilities

Lorraine Ruggieri

Abstract: *This article describes the underlying theories and the development of a mutual aid group for college freshman students with learning disabilities. The group, named Balancing It All, represented an attempt to construct a community in which learning disabilities could be normalized and a feeling of positivity and well-being could emerge through the combination of the compatible methodologies of strengths-based group practice and academic coaching.*

Keywords: *mutual aid group, learning disabilities, strengths-based group practice, academic coaching*

Introduction

As more and more students are diagnosed and treated in grade school with learning disabilities, increasing numbers of them will enter postsecondary institutions requesting services and accommodations as provided by Section 504 of the U.S. Federal Rehabilitation Act of 1973 In 1984, Ann Orzek, a mental health clinician, acknowledged the twofold obligation of postsecondary administrators to provide reasonable services and accommodations requested by students with learning disabilities while assessing their needs in order to create programs to better serve the increasing numbers of these students. Orzek proposed that peer support groups could provide opportunity for students with learning disabilities to have viable discussions for gaining support and for developing effective coping skills (Orzek, 1984).

This paper will discuss group work practice, as touted by Ann Orzek and supported by subsequent research, as an additional intervention to traditional medical treatments or educational interventions offered as accommodations to help students with learning disabilities who sought assistance from the Academic Access Program at Marymount Manhattan College in New York City. It will also document the development of a group work initiative, Balancing It All, and its results.

The Academic Access Program: A college service providing tutoring, accommodations and support

The Academic Access Program (AAP), a service for a fee-above-tuition, offers individual tutoring for students with learning disabilities. For two hours each week, a qualified learning specialist addresses the student's academic requirements, provides valuable assistance with course assignments and research papers, and keeps the student on track and productive. Additionally, for those who submit appropriate documentation of a learning disability, the program makes arrangements for such accommodations as extended test time, a separate test space, a note taker, use of a computer and/or assistive technology. Academic coaching, which encourages goal identification, motivation, autonomy and self-determination, time management, and the cultivation of executive function skills (i.e., cognitive skills needed to plan, organize and strategize goal -directed behavior), has been recently added as a new dimension of the AAP. Academic coaching, also called executive function coaching, serves as an adjunct to and augmentation of the tutoring assistance.

The group initiative

As an outgrowth of academic coaching, a mutual aid group was initiated, combining the merits of strengths-based social group work practice and academic coaching techniques. Called *Balancing It All,* this group initiative for freshman students with learning disabilities who participate in the AAP, was inaugurated in the spring semester of 2011. Its mission was to construct a community, a safe haven, where students with learning disabilities or disorders could normalize their concerns and develop a feeling of positivity and well-being. To fully explicate and demonstrate this group work initiative, there were four main objectives: (1) to explore the theory and application of multidisciplinary concepts from the fields of psychology, education, and social work as related to group work practice with students with learning disabilities; (2) to consider group work practice as an added layer of support for students with learning disabilities, particularly for freshman students who may feel isolated and marginal in the college community; (3) to demonstrate the potential for group work practice within the AAP's mission of providing tutoring, accommodations and support for students with learning disabilities; and (4) to present the development and results of the group initiative.

Theory and application of multidisciplinary concepts: Adolescent behavior described and diagnosed within a medical model framework

For the adolescent progressing towards maturity and adulthood, turbulent times are nearly routine and to be expected. As early as 1904, G. Stanley Hall (n.d.), psychologist, educator, and first president of Clark University, coined the phrase "storm and stress" in regard to adolescent development after extensive research and theorizing about this stage in human development. Hall identified three behavioral components within this period of development: *conflict with parents, mood disruptions,* and *risky behavior* (n.d.). Hence, the first descriptors of adolescent development are within a framework of a psychological, albeit nascent, medical model that denotes disturbance.

If adolescent development in general denotes a faulty pattern of behavior resulting from disturbance, one might expect that the development of adolescents with learning disabilities already challenged by their disorder would exhibit even more intense pathology and disturbances. It is within late adolescence that students with learning disabilities, as newly inducted college students, begin to deal with and respond to their emerging adulthood, academic responsibilities, and independence. Moreover, these students experience higher levels of stress and lower levels of adaptability (Heiman, 2006).

Students with learning disabilities – including attention deficit disorder (ADD), attention deficit/hyperactivity disorder (ADHD), and other learning and developmental disorders – are classified within a category of childhood and adolescent disorders as defined by certain criteria in the *Diagnostic and Statistical Manual of Mental Disorders*, Fourth Edition (DSM-IV). These criteria identify significant, chronic, or persistent disturbances that impair functioning (American Psychiatric Association, 2000) and are necessary to guide treatment to alleviate symptoms. Adhering to the medical model ideology of treatment for an impaired person, learning disorders, particularly ADD/ADHD, are generally treated with specific medications such as Ritalin, Adderall, Concerta, or Yvvance. This treatment attends to immediate relief of the primary symptoms (distractibility, impulsivity, and restlessness) but does not provide long-term manageability of the secondary effects of these disorders (noted below).

Learning disorders and their etiology described within the social constructionist theory

In 1997, social worker James E. Levine endorsed the etiology of ADHD from a social constructionist or person-in-environment perspective, observing that ADHD, a neurologically-based developmental disorder, "is assessed in terms of a particular constellation of symptoms, including problems with attention and persistence, impulsivity, and motor agitation" He noted that problem-laden descriptors – *"symptoms, deficits, handicaps"* – are "devoid of any considerations of the context in which symptoms occur" (Levine, 1997, p.199). This diagnosis usually called for a particular medication, which in turn, "verifies the diagnosis" so that a medical intervention will predominate at the expense of a more comprehensive and less physically invasive intervention (p.201).

Levine noted that ADHD, the most prevalent diagnosis for students with learning disabilities, had become an overarching term for the classification of a myriad of symptoms for all developmental and behavioral problems noted in the DSM- IV. Within this classification, there is little regard for understanding the student's history and context of symptoms. Rather than engage in reflection, interventions are narrow with little attention paid to long-term implications. Schools often segregate students with ADHD thus diminishing chances for interactions with peers throughout their school years and into later adult years. The secondary symptoms of these disabilities and disorders – feelings of disconnectedness, low self-esteem, stigma, social maladaptation or ineptness, and resentment – develop and internalize as loneliness, shame, and self-directed blame. In a nutshell, these students believe that there is a something gravely wrong with them and may not recognize their own strengths. Levine correlates this attention to disability which dominates school discourse with the medical model perspective. He puts forth and explores a more considerate constructionist theory inclusive of social work values (Levine, 1997).

Without consideration of social work values – service, social justice, dignity and worth of the person, importance of human relationships, integrity, and competence (NASW, 2011) – as a possible starting point for understanding and constructing an etiology of learning disorders, treatments are limited to fixing a problem within the confines of the medical model perspective with short term results.

Academic model broadened to include psychosocial interventions

In the academic and pedagogical model, educators teach and instruct students who follow their instruction. Tutors will correct errors, provide answers and provide instruction on note taking, test-taking and other learning strategies (Parker & Boutelle, 2009). The vast area of strengths, weaknesses, and compromised executive function skills may be unattended or not addressed. Though it may be an uphill battle, consideration of the psychosocial constructs of the problems of students with learning disabilities opens one up to the possibility of additional interventions, such as supportive counseling, academic coaching, and group work practice to afford students with learning disabilities a fully comprehensive spectrum of assistance. These additional interventions, particularly group work practice, can help students counter the secondary effects of learning disabilities – feelings of disconnectedness, accompanying stigma, social maladaptation or ineptness, and resentment – which they may suffer along with academic shortcomings. Optimistically, social group work practice, as a reflective and empowering intervention, may combat the societal constructs that contribute to the inhibitions and vulnerability of students with learning disabilities and which may in turn compromise learning ability and optimal achievement. Although there are few research studies from a social work stance utilizing psychosocial constructs, group work practice with students with learning disabilities remains to be implemented and tested. As the social constructionist theory implies, consideration of societal and environmental influences might help to attenuate the secondary effects of learning disabilities and may provide remedy for longer lasting lifestyle management of symptoms.

Group work practice as an added layer of support for students with learning disabilities: Interventions evolving from modifications of past theory

How can group work practice provide an added layer of support for students with learning disabilities challenged by the impairments of their disorder, the ramifications of a medical diagnosis of having something wrong with them and the limitations of social constructs? And what can ease any accompanying feelings of stigma, isolation, and marginalization? These are daunting questions. Perhaps answers are evolving and emerging from modifications of past theory.

Though we have advanced more than a century from Stanley Hall's early work on adolescence, the disease model for adolescent disturbances still dominates the helping professions that seek to offer therapy and treatment. However, progress has been made.

In 2001, the Learning Disabilities Association of Ontario, Canada, defined learning disabilities as impairments in psychological processing that impact learning in those of average or above average intelligence and are separate from intellectual impairments (The Learning Disabilities Association of Ontario, 2001). Students with learning disabilities have the potential to excel but fall short and may experience feelings of anxiety, poor performance in college classes and a general feeling of ineptness. By broadening the scope of interventions to include mutual aid groups for these students, social skills and individual strengths might be enhanced and may accompany academic achievement. Orzek, previously mentioned above, applied the fundamental theories of Arthur Chickering (Chickering, 1969) on vectors of development for college students (developing purpose, autonomy, competence, integrity, managing emotions, establishing identity and freeing interpersonal relationships) to the special concerns of students with learning disabilities and suggested that they may be addressed in a peer support group. This possibility might further be pursued through the integration of various overlapping approaches from the fields of education (academic or executive function coaching), social work practice (strength-based orientation, social constructionist theory), and the emerging field of positive psychology (extracting positive qualities). Co-mingled with group work practice, a peer support group might be devised that would develop empowerment, a feeling of community and connectedness with others, the ability to deal with stress factors, and the promotion of mutual aid, well-being and positivity.

Academic coaching and peer support groups enhance coping techniques

Academic coaching has emerged within the last decade as an effective approach to enhance academic success providing support for the development of the skills, strategies and mindset necessary for students with learning disabilities to manage executive function challenges dealing with time management, motivation, and the ability to regulate and organize behavior. Tasks are undertaken collaboratively with the academic coach and the student in a partnership that strongly promotes the student's autonomy. The academic coach bolsters the student's strengths helping each student to develop his or her own strategies and tools to optimize academic achievement. (Parker & Boutelle, 2009).

To this end, the coach must hone his or her own basic counseling and communication skills of active listening, reflecting, questioning and empathizing. (Schwartz, Prevatt & Proctor, 2005). Similarly, in group work practice, a group facilitator encourages group members to work collaboratively, employs questions as a tool for inspiring meaningful group discussion, and focuses on empowerment from within one's own capacity. The group facilitator also employs communication skills of listening, reflecting, questioning, and empathizing. In similar ways, guided by either a coach or a facilitator, academic coaching and mutual aid groups activate and encourage student's potential in developing coping techniques.

Strength-based group work to combat the secondary symptoms of learning disabilities

There are further benefits to the development of this methodology of combining strength- based group work and techniques of academic coaching. Oftentimes, students report feelings of depression and isolation, self-consciousness, and, in some cases, self-loathing to the academic coach. Privately, they either deny or shield themselves from those feelings by avoidance behaviors (e.g., missing classes, procrastination, last-minute unedited papers, incompletes), which add to the problems of exclusion and undercurrents of stigma. Strengths-based group work can draw these students together in camaraderie to collaboratively identify these feelings, gain support, foster feelings of empowerment, and learn from those who will accept them in this new community. As group facilitators, we employ the process of group building to promote a sense of community. "Essentially, we do it by helping them identify those issues, needs, concerns, desires and goals that will bind them as a community" and "to help group members come to feel a sense of their *we-ness*" (Steinberg, 2004, p.25). Additionally, with guidance from the facilitator and the academic coach, a spirit of *I can do* becomes amplified by all who are *in the same boat* (community). Through the discovery of mutual goals and desires, the *same-boat* dynamic develops and strengthens mutual aid (Steinberg, 2004).

Positive psychology and the promotion of well-being

Enhancement of learning abilities and potential for developing coping strategies for the deficits of learning disabilities may be seen as a positive intervention that fosters a pro-active methodology for achievement and well-being. In a recent study, "students experienced coaching as a transformational process that enhanced their overall well-being and allowed them to develop positive expectations about their futures" (Parker & Boutelle, 2009, p.211). When this perspective is incorporated in a mutual aid group, students in a group can begin to visualize the good life in the spirit of positive psychology, a vision articulated by the social and behavioral sciences (Seligman & Csikszentmihalyi, 2000, p.5). The secondary effects of learning disabilities are attenuated and new social constructs are formed within a group experience.

Potential for group work practice within the AAP

From a theoretical perspective, incorporation of group work practice into the AAP can add valuable opportunities for students with learning disabilities to supplement their studies with the development of coping skills and responsible behaviors. They will learn strategies for independence (developing an internal locus) and interdependence (share concerns and solutions, study groups) that will allow for the developmental shift from dependency on parents to interdependency with peers (Orzek, 1984).

It was easy to make a case that there is a place for group work practice as an adjunct to traditional methods for treatment and tools for achievement utilized by students with learning disabilities as well as by other students in the AAP who cope with brain or developmental disorders (e.g., epilepsy, traumatic brain injury, Asperger's disorder, dyslexia, and dysgraphia) and who seek tutoring, accommodations, and academic coaching.

A group initiative as part of the ongoing tutoring, academic advisement and accommodations services available to the AAP was therefore initiated in the spring 2011 semester. With this addition, as well as assistive technology and academic coaching, the AAP operated at full capacity of 40 students, 13 of whom were freshmen.

Balancing it all: Development

My aspirations for group work practice for students with learning disabilities participating in the AAP in the spring of 2011 were to incorporate basic values and principles such as empathy and respect for all, non-judgmental attitude, employment of a strengths-based perspective, inclusiveness of all needs, and commitment and responsibility to the work. The principles I hoped to utilize in group process were purposeful use of self, authenticity, collaboration, turning back to the group, thinking group, sharing group authority, free-form interaction and advancing a positive psychology. Attempting to perpetuate these earnest intentions and principles motivated me to thoroughly engage and understand the challenges of students with learning disabilities and to facilitate *Balancing It All* incorporating empathetic interventions.

Pre-planning

Previous research from the University of Iowa endorsed support groups as a preferred practice in serving students with ADD (Richard, 1995, #13), but with few details. *The Handbook of Social Work with Groups* provided an informative chapter by Andrew Malekoff (2006) that introduced a framework for strengths-based group work with children and adolescents. Malekoff stressed the importance of clarity of group purpose and individual needs for effective groups with adolescents with ADD and ADHD and warned that sweeping negative generalizations – "the literature states that groups don't work for ADD kids" – are "rarely helpful" (Malekoff, p.232).

Considering these pronouncements, *Balancing It All* was conceptualized as an all gender group for freshman students in the AAP who had expressed interest in joining a support group. Its purpose was clearly stated and embraced by all in individual pre-group meetings. A pre-planning model following the advice and format of Roselle Kurland in *Group Formation: A Guide to the Development of Successful Groups* (Kurland, 1982) was developed to address the needs of the group; the needs of individual members; the needs of the program; and the needs of the worker with clarity and definition of purpose.

Group needs

To provide group support in an interactive and confidential environment for students with learning disabilities to meet, share experiences, gain information and mutual aid.

Individual needs

In personal interviews before the group began and in the first group meeting, the participants discussed their individual needs concerning these issues: concern about meeting the rigorous schedule of college life, fear of failure, socializing and building a network of friends, desire to please parents, ambivalent feelings toward gaining independence and coping with overwhelming stress and anxiety.

Needs of the program

Prior to the inception of the group, the parents of students in the AAP had requested the services of an academic coach. Thus, the group initiative was an offspring of academic coaching and was sanctioned by the director of the program and parents as an additional layer of support for these students to ease their transition into college life.

Worker needs

To facilitate a group in a flexible and purposeful manner and to develop a leadership role that was collaborative and that provided for dynamic group process and allowed mutual aid to develop.

The Purpose of the Group: Balancing it all

The purpose of the group was to help freshman students in the AAP adjust to college life, to share feelings and to receive support. The goals of the group would be to foster engagement and empowerment, to process and integrate new identities, to meet new responsibilities and to receive and give mutual aid.

Membership

Group membership consisted initially of two male and three female freshman students in the AAP who were being tutored individually by the program's learning specialists. Membership remained open. Commonality existed due to inclusion in the college community and AAP and a documented history of learning disabilities such as ADD, ADHD, dyslexia, and dysgraphia. In addition, some of the students experienced impairments resulting from brain cancer, Asperger's disorder, and epilepsy. Differences existed due to individual personalities, background and upbringing, ethnicities, impact of learning disabilities, parental support and reactions to the students' disabilities, ongoing medical care, use of medication, reactions to challenges, and individual goals/interests.

Group structure

The group was structured to meet for one hour on six Wednesday afternoons. Consecutive weekly meetings were impossible due to days off for special events, advisement days, examinations, unavailability of a meeting place and changes in class schedules. Additionally, there were limitations on available meeting times because of the varied schedules of the students. Meetings were to be held in the AAP director's office which she would vacate for the group meeting. All attempts to acquire another meeting space at the college were unsuccessful due to lack of space.

A major goal for the initial meeting was to establish the group as a safe place for the students to express themselves to one another. Northen and Kurland (2001) state that group members often fear that a worker may violate their right to privacy and reveal information. Therefore, the worker must assure the members that information about them will not be shared outside of the group and that members are to adhere to this rule. Confidentiality was part of the group contract and was repeatedly stressed at each meeting. An agreed upon provision was that the program director may be informed of the content of the meetings. This condition is also expressed by Northen and Kurland (2001) who state that members may expect that some information may be shared within the agency.

Group content

Mindful of the constructionist theory that underscores the need for eliciting the client's story, group content was initially a sharing of histories, assisting the member to see the socially constructed nature of problems and helping the participant to envision possibilities of overcoming challenges (Parker, 1997). However, students were slow to engage in revealing individual histories and preferred to remain in the *here and now*. Group participants were eager to vent on current situations rather than reflect; they sought concrete immediate solutions with regard to their challenges. Therefore, the therapeutic intent of a constructionist view – "a humanistic one, because it invites communal self-reflection rather than emphasis on individual deficiency" (Parker, 1997, p.205) – remained on hold.

Discussions were free form and stressed the attitudes and feelings shared regarding interests, concerns, needs, fears, anxieties, and pursuits. The norms, themes and expectations of college life in comparison to previous high school experiences were noted and new identities as college students were explored along with patterns of interaction between other students and faculty. As events transpired – midterm exams, death of a grandparent, poor grades, indecision over major, desire to find a job – reflection and insight were deflected in preference to attention to exigencies.

Results

Balancing It All had disheartening results and fell short of its goal to create a community for students with learning disabilities. Practice did not conform to theory and fell far short of the desired results. As such, these were my observations:

- A group without a recurring scheduled place to meet is like a building without a foundation; it easily falls apart. Due to the unavailability and undependability of space to meet – sharing the director's office was limiting – a safe haven may never have been established. Students failed to show up consistently for meetings and drifted away.
- Intervening and/or unplanned events and changes in class schedules caused groups to be cancelled. This instability hampered group formation and cohesiveness.
- Facebook became a suitable societal construct for connecting with other students. Students immediately exchanged Facebook information at the first group meeting to connect with each other; they may have preferred to construct their own separate community electronically.
- Initial resistance to a group experience was never overcome. Though students joined the group voluntarily, several expressed ambivalent and/or negative feelings regarding other groups in which they had participated. Some had been placed in mandatory groups for "slow" students and claimed to have planned pranks to sabotage group process.
- The purpose of the group, though clearly stated, was interpreted to

be remedial and not empowering. Connecting with one's strengths and empowerment was overshadowed by a feeling of being in a classification shared by others with weaknesses. As a result students lost interest before exploring the group's benefits.

• Group norms or rules were sometimes questioned and breached by students. Confidentiality, though stressed repeatedly, was considered not possible to adhere to. Participants revealed past experiences when they engaged in gossip or were the object of gossip because the content of group discussions was revealed outside of group meetings.

• Social support from peers is an important protective factor for a student's adjustment to a college setting (Heiman & Kariv, 2004). However, supportive behavior can be misinterpreted by college students who may be eager to develop intimate relationships with other group members. Social cues can be misunderstood and feelings of anger and hostility may result if advances are rejected. Delicate situations arise when there is a sexual attraction between group members that is not mutual; as a result participants fled. This behavior was noted in the group.

Conclusion

College life may appear to be a muddle for students with learning disabilities. The impairments of their disorder and feelings of stigma, shame, depression, and futility may diminish ability for academic success and satisfaction. But there is hope and help.

Medical and educational models provide assistance for these students in specific ways – medication, tutoring, coaching, accommodations, assistive technology, etc. – geared to the individual. Psychosocial interventions in the form of social group work may provide additional assistance to students by helping them identify and develop their strengths, support systems, and coping skills. Though group work practice did not achieve a *goodness of fit* with these freshman students with learning disabilities, they evaluated the group meetings as *satisfying* and stated that they would be willing to try again. As group facilitator and academic coach, one might reconsider group purpose for these students and form a group that is task or activity oriented with emphasis on individual and group strengths and teamwork. Mutual aid and empowerment might develop well in these types of group. Workshops, fundraisers, theme parties/events are all possibilities for future groups. Also, flexibility is the most important skill to develop when facilitating a group with students with learning disabilities and dealing with their exigencies. In addition, it is important to remedy the shortcomings of this group initiative when it is retooled with attention to social group work fundamentals. Meeting regularly in a consistent place, teaching about the importance of trust and confidentiality, allowing group members to form the agenda and be self-directed, and discussing taboo topics such as sexual attraction and rejection will enhance groups for students with disabilities.

References

American Psychiatric Association, (2000). *Diagnostic and statistical manual of mental Disorders, text revision (DSM-IV-TR)*, (*4th ed.*). Washington, DC: Author.

Chickering, A.W. (1969). Education and identity. San Francisco: Jossey-Bass.

Hall, G. Stanley,(n.d.). In *New World Encyclopedia online*. Retrieved March 29, 2011 from http://www.newworldencyclopedia.org/entry/G._Stanley_Hall

Heiman, T. & Kariv, D. (2004). Coping experience among students in higher education. *Educational Studies, 30* (4), 441-455.

Heiman, T. (2006). Social support networks, stress, sense of coherence and academic success of university students with learning disabilities. *Social Psychology of Education*, 9, 461-478.

Kurland, R. (1982). *Group formation: a guide to the development of successful groups*, Kinney, T. & Loavenbruck, G. (Eds.) United Neighborhood Centers of America, Inc. and Continuing Education Program School of Social Welfare, Nelson A. Rockefeller Center of Public Affairs and Policy, State University of New York at Albany,1-20.

Levine, J. (1997). Re-visioning attention deficit hyperactivity disorder (ADHD). *Clinical Social Work Journal*, 25 (2), 197-209.

Malekoff, A. (2006). Strengths-based group work with children and adolescents. In C. Garvin, L. Gutierrez & M. Galinsky (Eds.), *Handbook of social work with groups* (pp. 227-244). New York: The Guilford Press.

NASW (2011). Retrieved April 22, 2011 from http://www.socialworkers.org/pubs/code/code.asp

Northen, H. & Kurland, R. (2001). *Social work with groups*, 3rd ed. NYC: Columbia University Press.

Orzek, A. (1984). Special needs of the learning disabled college student: Implications fo interventions through peer support groups. *The Personnel and Guidance Journal, 62* (7), 404-407.

Parker, D. & Boutelle, K. (2009). Executive function coaching for college students with learning disabilities and ADHD: a new approach for fostering self-determination. *Learning Disabilities Research & Practice, 24*(4), 204-215.

Richard, M.M. (1995). Pathways to success for the college student with ADD accommodations and preferred practices. *Journal of Postsecondary Education and Disability, 11*(2&3), unnumbered.

Schwartz, S., Prevatt, F. & Proctor, B. (2005). A coaching intervention for college students with Attention deficit/hyperactivity disorder. *Psychology in the Schools, 42*(6), 647-656.

Seligman, M.E.P., & Csikszentmihalyi, M. (Eds.) (2000). Positive psychology: an introduction. *American Psychologist, 55*(1), 5-14.

Seligman, M.E.P., Steen, T., Park, N. & Peterson, C. (2005). Positive psychology progress: Empirical validation of interventions. *American Psychologist, 60*(5), 410-421.

Steinberg, D.M. (2004). *The mutual aid approach to working with groups: Helping people help one another.* New York: The Haworth Press.

The Learning Disabilities Association of Ontario (2001). Retrieved on May 4, 2013 from website: http://www.ldao.ca/documents/Definition_and_Suporting%20Document_2001.pdf

6

Using a reflecting team as a small group exercise in the social work classroom

W. J. Casstevens and Marcia Cohen

Abstract: *Reflecting teams were developed in the postmodern, constructionist environment of narrative therapy, and have been used as both a clinical and a training tool, as well as in graduate education in business schools. The authors have applied this as a small group approach to developing critical thinking and collaboration in the social work classroom. To be successful, the reflecting team needs to demonstrate critical thinking in discussion amongst team members, yet at the same time needs to avoid being negative. Student participants in two social work courses reported an increased ability both to see issues from the perspective of others, and to critically reflect upon their own process.*

Keywords: *reflecting team, group work, reflective learning, critical thinking, narrative therapy*

Introduction

Reflecting teams developed in the postmodern, constructionist environment of narrative therapy, embedded in systems theory and family therapy. Andersen developed the reflecting team approach in family therapy (Brownlee, Vis, & McKenna, 2009) and it has since been used as both a clinical and a teaching tool (Griffith, 1999; Kleist, 1999; Wahlstroem, 2006). Cox, Bañez, Hawley, and Mostade (2003) recommended using reflecting teams for training group workers in classroom settings. They suggested two formats for classroom exercises noting "that there could be many variations of this process and that it could be used in a variety of situations (Anderson, 1991, 1995)" (Cox, et al., p. 104). This is perhaps not surprising, since reflecting teams are themselves small groups.

The authors applied this small group approach to developing critical thinking and collaboration in the social work classroom, and evaluated these reflecting team exercises through anonymous student questionnaires. This chapter presents reflecting teams, reflective learning, and an approach to formatting reflecting team exercises in human behavior and group work classrooms. It also reports results from student feedback questionnaires that were used to evaluate these classroom exercises.

The reflecting team in therapy

As used in therapy, the reflecting team model consists of a three-step sequence: (a) Client – Therapist interaction, (b) Listening/Reflecting Consultants interaction, and (c) Client – Therapist interaction resumes, and Client reacts to the Consultants' interaction (Griffith, 1999). In this model, the Listening/Reflecting Consultants comprise the reflecting team. In narrative therapy, if either therapeutic discourse reaches an impasse, or widening their audience would benefit clients, a reflecting team may be invited into a therapy session (Monk, 1997). Team members are generally selected through therapist-client consultation: "A reflecting team/audience may consist of individuals who are family/ friends to the client or strangers to the client, e.g., colleagues or interns of the client's therapist and/or relevant other specialists such as a priest or minister; or members of the community who have been through similar experiences (White, 2007)" (Taliaferro, Casstevens, & Decuir-Gunby, 2013).

The carefully selected reflecting team members observe session dialog, then the therapist and client remove themselves to observe the team as it reflects on the observed interaction. After this occurs, the team departs and client and therapist resume their session. It is hoped that reflecting team input will result in a shift in the client system, that is, in change (O'Connor, Davis, Meakes, Pickering, & Schuman, 2004; Wahlstroem, 2006).

Brownlee, Vis, and McKenna (2009) challenged researchers to further examine the effectiveness of this model, as it involves extensive use of time and resources on behalf of clients. Both Kleist (1999) and Brownlee et al., (2009) while recommending further research, agreed that the evidence on the use of reflecting teams in family and couple counseling by and large supports the model's continued use. Griffith (1999) expanded the model's application, and used reflecting teams in the classroom as "an alternative case teaching model" (p. 343) in graduate level business education.

Reflective learning in professional education

Reflective learning plays an important part in professional education in a variety of disciplines, including social work. Platzer, Blake, and Ashford (2000), for example, evaluated reflective learning in nursing education, using reflective practice groups that "enabled some of the students to develop their critical thinking and professionalism" (p. 694). Platzer et al. (2000) suggested that group work "could further enhance a learner's opportunities to consider different viewpoints and reflect on their own experiences" (p. 691). Charalambous (2003) agreed that reflection can facilitate teaching, pointing out that it "has increasingly become a cornerstone of nursing professionalism" (p. 1 of 8), and connecting it to "helping students learn about and from clinical experience" (p. 3 of 8). Although Charalambous discussed counseling in the context of reflection, narrative therapy and reflecting teams were not mentioned. In social work education, Noble (2001) and Rai (2006) explored reflective writing and student narratives. Rai noted that: "Reflection remains at the core of social work education, although its face may have evolved" (p. 795). Holland and Kilpatrick's (1993) work with using narrative analysis and reflective questions to teach a multicultural approach to practice is yet another example of how narrative and reflection have been used in social work education. Incorporating reflecting team activities within the social work classroom could be viewed as one more step in this evolution.

Classroom implementation

The first author of this article introduced the reflecting team into an undergraduate classroom in an experiential exercise on group work: The instructor took the role of group leader or facilitator, student volunteers participated as members in the group process, and a panel of observers (the remainder of the class) watched the group, then discussed their observations among themselves while the group members and leader observed. This exercise was enthusiastically received. The first author then used a reflecting team activity in a small graduate level class, again as an experiential exercise on group work. In this situation, however, student volunteers requested a follow-up dialog to process the observers' reflection, and class ran overtime attending to this request. Anecdotally, both BSW and MSW students found these reflecting teams to be engaging and constructive aids to experiencing and reflecting on the use of groups in social work practice. This informal feedback led the authors to more systematically evaluate the usefulness of reflecting team activities in social work classrooms. Griffith (1999) explicitly adapted the reflecting team model for use in the classroom, and summarized six major rules for reflection as guidelines for student use (a slightly modified version of these is provided in Figure 1). The authors used the modified guidelines to help standardize the process for reflecting team activities in this study.

Method

The authors used Griffith's (1999; see Figure 1 overleaf) reflecting team approach in two social work courses (a total of three course sections) at two universities, as part of a broader study that had Institutional Review Board approval at the first author's university. The courses were graduate level, semester-long courses; one of the courses was group work specific. The group work specific course was an advanced level practice course with two sections (*Social Work Practice with Groups*; n = 14 and n = 17, respectively). Each section of *Social Work Practice with Groups* incorporated two reflecting team activities during the semester. The other course was a foundation level human behavior course with one section (*Human Behavior & the Social Environment: Individuals, Families, & Groups*; n = 21). The human behavior course incorporated three reflecting team activities during the semester. Because of the larger class size (n = 21), two process group/reflecting team dyads convened concurrently to allow all students to participate

Figure 1. Reflecting Team Activity Handout Paraphrased from Griffith (1999).

Guidelines for consultations (based on Griffith, 1999):

1. Restrict speculations to conversations that take place during the activity in this room today
2. Present ideas tentatively, e.g., starting with "I was wondering..." or "perhaps..."
3. Comments are to be positive or logical, rather than negative or blaming
4. Share perceptions without evaluation, judgment, or explanation/ justification of team member perceptions
5. Attempt to present both sides of any dilemma, moving from "either-or" to a "both-and" position
6. Maintain eye contact with fellow team members during the team consultation

in each of the three activities.

Anonymous in-class questionnaires administered at the end-of-semester were used to evaluate the impact of reflecting team activities (see Figure 2). The questionnaires offered three identical questions; the *Practice with Groups* questionnaire added two questions, and the *Human Behavior* questionnaire added one question. For the *Practice with Groups* course the added questions (1) related to group process and facilitation, and (2) asked whether this was a useful format. For the *Human Behavior* course the added question related to students' abilities to see things from the perspective of others.

The instructor provided students with a handout of Griffith's (1999) slightly modified guidelines (Figure 1) for reference during each reflecting team activity. In order to address any sensitive feelings that might surface, the instructors also added a fourth step to the reflecting team classroom activity. This led to the following small group format: (1) Small Group – Facilitator interaction; (2) Reflecting Team interaction; (3) Small Group – Facilitator interaction resumes and reacts to the Reflecting Team interaction; (4) Reflecting Team interaction resumes and reacts to the second Small Group – Facilitator interaction.

In the classroom, instructors had students divide into small groups of 5 – 8 students each, which became (1) a process group, and (2) a reflecting team. The process group facilitator was either selected by

Figure 2. Anonymous End-of-Semester Questionnaires.

Human Behavior	Practice with Groups
Recall the 3 Reflecting Team exercises, focusing on what defines social class, teen suicide and sexual orientation, and aging and care-giving. Did the Reflecting Team format contribute to the enhancement or development of your: ___ Yes ___ No Critical thinking skills ___ Yes ___ No Small group collaboration ___ Yes ___ No Ability to see issues from the perspective of others ___ Yes ___ No Ability to critically reflect upon your own process Please explain below: Thank you for your feedback on this type of group exercise!!	Recall the 2 Reflecting Team exercises, focusing on the role plays. Did the Reflecting Team format contribute to the enhancement or development of your: ___ Yes ___ No Critical thinking skills ___ Yes ___ No Small group collaboration ___ Yes ___ No Awareness of group process and group facilitation ___ Yes ___ No Ability to critically reflect upon your own process ___ Yes ___ No Do you think this was a useful format? Please explain below: Thank you for your feedback on this type of group exercise!!

group members or assigned by the instructor. The process group was provided either with a role-play scenario (in the group work course), or with structured questions on current course material for discussion (in the human behavior course). During the ensuing small group activity, the reflecting team observed and took notes. The groups then switched places, and the reflecting team discussed what it observed, with appropriate related commentary that followed the handout guidelines "major rules for reflection" (Griffith, 1999, p. 354-355; refer to Table 1). Finally, the original process group reconvened and concluded the exercise, discussing group members' thoughts and/or feelings on the reflecting team's discussion and commentary.

Each group segment took between 10 and 20 minutes (segment lengths were determined in advance, so students knew what to expect). The entire exercise initially took about one hour and 15 minutes, including the initial explanation, coaching, and group formation. Once students were familiar with the guidelines for the activity, a reflecting team exercise could be completed in approximately one hour.

The way a reflecting team handles its comments is central to the success of any reflecting team exercise. In the classroom, for example, while demonstrating critical thinking in role plays and/or discussion amongst team members, reflecting teams also need to avoid negativity. This has an added benefit of making reflecting teams excellent experiential exercises in strengths-based discourse.

Results

Responses from the anonymous questionnaires for each class are tabulated for reference (Table 1.1, Table 1.2 and Table 2). The group work students were second year MSW students at a medium-sized private university in the American northeast. In Section 1 of the *Practice with Groups* course, 12 of the 14 students responded for a response rate of 85.7% (see Table 1.1). All respondents reported that the reflecting team exercises contributed to the enhancement or development of their critical thinking skills. Ninety-two percent reported that this was a useful format, and the exercises contributed to the enhancement or development of their ability to critically reflect upon their own process. Eighty-three percent reported that the exercises enhanced their awareness of group process and facilitation. Finally, 75% reported that the reflecting team exercises contributed to the enhancement or development of group collaboration.

In Section 2 of the *Practice with Groups* course, 14 of 17 students responded for a response rate of 82.4% (see Table 1.2). All respondents reported that the reflecting team exercises contributed to the enhancement or development of their awareness of group process and facilitation, though only 57% reported the exercises contributed to the enhancement or development of group collaboration. Ninety-three percent reported that this was a useful format; 86% reported the exercises contributed to the enhancement or development of their critical thinking skills; and 79% reported it contributed to their ability to critically reflect upon their own process.

Students in both course sections provided comments. In Section 1 of *Practice with Groups*, three students (25%) commented on the

Table 1.1 Social Work Practice with Groups – Section 1.

Question n = 12	Yes	No
Critical thinking skills	12 (100%)	0
Small group collaboration	9 (75%)	3 (25%)
Awareness of group process and facilitation	10 (83%) 1(8%) "somewhat"	1 (8%)
Ability to critically reflect on own process	11 (92%) 1(8%) "somewhat"	0
Useful format?	11 (92%) 1(8%) "somewhat"	0

Table 1.2 Social Work Practice with Groups – Section 2.

Question n = 14	Yes	No
Critical thinking skills	12 (86%)	2 (14%)
Small group collaboration	8 (57%) 1 (7%) "maybe"	5 (36%)
Awareness of group process and facilitation	14 (100%)	0
Ability to critically reflect on own process	11 (79%) 1(7%) "maybe"	2 (14%)
Useful format?	13 (93%)	1 (7%)

Table 2. Human Behavior and the Social Environment: Individuals, Families, and Groups.

Question n = 19	Yes	No
Critical thinking skills	10 (53%)	9 (47%)
Small group collaboration	17 (89%)	2 (11%)
Ability to see issues from perspective of others	15 (79%)	4 (21%)
Ability to critically reflect on own process	14 (74%)	5 (26%)

"lack of authenticity" involved with role-play scenarios. Two students (17%) requested more structure while one student (8%) suggested less (this student also commented on the format's helpfulness). In total, 10 of the 12 students (83.3%) commented on the helpfulness of the reflecting team exercises. In Section 2 of *Practice with Groups*, six students (43%) commented that doing this exercise when classmates were more comfortable with one another and/or with role-playing would have been less intimidating. In addition, seven of the 14 students (50%) commented on the helpfulness of the exercises. Two students (14%) commented that the reflecting team exercises were difficult to remember at the end of semester. (While it is possible these two students were absent during relevant class sessions, obtaining feedback immediately following class exercises – rather than at the end of the course – is suggested for future studies.) It may be mentioned that students in both sections of the group work course added notes to the yes/no options provided in the first five questions, writing in "somewhat" or "maybe" in response to some questions; these are noted on Tables 1.1 and 1.2. Overall, students in Section 1 of the group work course appeared to respond more favorably to the reflecting team activities than did students in Section 2.

In the human behavior class, 19 of 21 students responded to the questionnaire, for a response rate of 90.5% (see Table 2). These were first-year MSW students at a large southern state university. Eighty-nine percent of respondents reported that the reflecting team exercises contributed to the enhancement or development of group collaboration. Seventy-nine percent of respondents reported that the exercises contributed to the enhancement or development of their ability to see issues from the perspective of others, and 74% reported the exercises contributed to the enhancement or development of their ability to critically reflect upon their own process. However, only 53% of respondents reported the exercises contributed to the enhancement or development of critical thinking skills (discussed further below).

Students provided comments on the questionnaires. In the foundation level human behavior class, three of the 19 students (16%) commented that the reflecting team portion of the activity was not helpful, while seven students (37%) commented on its helpfulness. Four students (21%) commented that the second reflecting team process (Step 4) was unnecessary.

Discussion

Study limitations include the addition of course specific questions to the questionnaire that was used to obtain student feedback, and it is recommended that questionnaires used across courses be identical in future research. In addition, the questionnaires would optimally have been administered immediately following each reflecting team exercise. Although the intention was to reduce social desirability bias, waiting until the end of the course to administer the instrument may have led to diminished recollection of reflecting team exercises and their impact.

Some interesting differences in between-course responses were noted. An overall 65% of respondents in the two sections of the group work course (n = 26) reported that reflecting team exercises enhanced or developed small group collaboration, contrasting with the 89% of respondents in the human behavior course (n =21) who reported this. This marked difference may be due in part to the strong emphasis on small group collaboration that was present from day one in *Practice with Groups*. Since students were already accustomed to having this content emphasized, their perception of the proportionate contribution that reflecting team exercises made may have been less than it otherwise could have been. The human behavior course did not emphasize group collaboration as heavily, and these students may have perceived reflecting team experiences as contributing proportionately more to enhancing or developing group collaboration.

An overall 92% of respondents in the two sections of the group work course (n = 26) reported that reflecting team exercises enhanced or developed their critical thinking skills, which contrasts dramatically with the 53% of respondents in the human behavior course (n =21) who reported this. At the same time, 79% of respondents in the human behavior course reported that these exercises contributed to their ability to see issues from the perspective of others, and 74% reported these exercises contributed to their ability to critically reflect upon their own process. Paul and Elder (2010) defined critical thinking as "the art of analyzing and evaluating thinking with a view to improving it" (p. 2), a definition that would appear to include both seeing issues from multiple perspectives and critical self-reflection. While the concept "critical thinking" was explicitly discussed and defined during the group work course, this did not occur during the human behavior course. It is possible that the human behavior students did not interpret the term as was intended – to remedy this in subsequent human behavior classes the instructor has added a presentation on critical thinking that is followed by class discussion.

Although this was a relatively small study with accompanying limitations, the authors find it had distinct implications for teaching. Almost all of the students viewed the reflecting team exercises as beneficial to their learning. In terms of lessons for the future, results suggest that this activity should not be undertaken without a prior discussion of critical thinking and self-reflection, to familiarize students with these concepts before engaging them in reflecting team exercises. The feeling of intimidation expressed by some of the *Practice with Groups* Section 2 students suggests a need for instructors to be sensitive to the level of class cohesion, co-creating with students a sense of safety and mutuality in the classroom before introducing reflecting team exercises. Comments from human behavior students that the reflecting team's second round of reflection (i.e., Step 4) was unnecessary would appear to support this suggestion, particularly given this human behavior class was a cohesive entity prior to its first reflecting team exercise.

Implications for group work education

The social group work education literature has consistently emphasized the importance of experiential teaching and learning (Berger, 1996; Birnbaum, 1984; Cohen, 1996; Dennison, 2005). Cohen (2011) found that a variety of experiential teaching methods have been used successfully to teach group work assessment and practice skills. Reflecting team exercises are a versatile teaching tool likely to benefit most social work students. Possible applications of this teaching tool in group work education include its use in: (a) role-playing, (b) addressing sensitive topics using open-ended questions as a focus for small group discussions, (c) enhancing critical thinking skills, and (d) providing experiential practice in strengths-based dialog. With any of these applications, the way the reflecting team handles its comments is central to the success of the exercise – the team needs to demonstrate critical thinking in discussion amongst team members, yet at the same time needs to remain strengths based. As discussed previously, student participants in two social work courses (two sections of *Practice with Groups* and one of *Human Behavior*) reported an increased ability to critically reflect upon their own process after participating in reflecting team activities.

References

Andersen, T. (Ed.) (1991). *The reflecting team: Dialogues and dialogues about the dialogues*. New York: Norton.

Anderson, T. (1995). Reflecting processes; acts of informing and forming: You can borrow my eyes, but you must not take them away from me! In S. Friedman (Ed.), *The reflecting team in action: Collaborative practice in family therapy* (pp. 11- 37). New York: Guilford.

Berger, R. (1996). A comparative analysis of different teaching methods of teaching group work. *Social Work with Groups, 19*(1), 79–89.

Birnbaum, M. L. (1984). The integration of didactic and experiential learning in the teaching of group work. *Journal of Education for Social Work, 20*, 50–58.

Brownlee, K., Vis, J., & McKenna, A. (2009). Review of the reflecting team process: Strengths, challenges, and clinical implications. *The Family Journal, 17*(2), 139-145.

Charalambous, A. (January – March, 2003). Reflective practice as a facilitator for learning. *ICUS NURS WEB J*, Issue 13, 1-8.

Cohen, M. B. (1996). Bringing the mountain to Mohammed: An experiential approach to teaching group dynamics in the classroom. In B. Stempler, M. Glass, & C. M Savinelli (Eds.), *Social group work today and tomorrow* (pp. 71–85). Binghamton, New York: Haworth Press.

Cohen, M. B. (2011). Using student task groups to teach group process and development. *Social Work with Groups*, 34(1), 51-60.

Cox, J. A., Bañez, L., Hawley, L. D., & Mostade, J. (2003). Use of the reflecting team process in the training of group workers, *Journal for Specialists in Group Work*, 28(2), 89-105.

Dennison, S. (2005). Enhancing the integration of group theory with practice: A five-part teaching strategy. *Journal of Baccalaureate Social Work, 10*(2), 53–68.

Griffith, W. (1999). The reflecting team model as an alternative case teaching model: A narrative conversational approach. *Management Learning,*

30(3), 343-362.

Holland, T. P., & Kilpatrick, A. C. (1993). Using Narrative Techniques to Enhance Multicultural Practice, *Journal of Social Work Education,* 29(3).

Kleist, D. M. (1999). Reflecting on the reflecting process: A research perspective. *The Family Journal,* 7(3), 270-275.

Monk, G. (1997). How narrative therapy works. In G. Monk, J. Winslade, K. Crocket, & D. Epston (Eds.). *Narrative therapy in practice: The archaeology of hope (pp. 331).* San Francisco: Jossey-Bass.

Noble, C. (2001). Researching field practice in social work education: Integration of theory and practice through the use of narratives. *Journal of Social Work,* 1(3), 347-360.

O'Connor, T. S., Davis, A., Meakes, E., Pickering, R., & Schuman, M. (2004). Narrative therapy using a reflecting team: An ethnographic study of therapists' experiences. *Contemporary Family Therapy,* 26(1), 23-39.

Paul, R., & Elder, L. (2009). *The miniature guide to critical thinking: Concepts and tools.* USA: Foundation for Critical Thinking Press.

Platzer, H., Blake, D., & Ashford, D. (2003). An evaluation of process and outcomes from learning through reflective practice groups on a post-registration nursing course. *Journal of Advanced Nursing,* 31(3), 689-695.

Rai, L. (2006). Owning (up to) reflective writing in social work education. *Social Work Education,* 25(8), 785-797.

Taliaferro, J. D., Casstevens, W. J., & DeCuir-Gunby, J. T. (2013). Working with African American clients using narrative therapy: An operational citizenship and critical race theory framework. *The International Journal of Narrative Therapy and Community Work,* 1, 34-45.

Wahlstroem, J. (2006). Narrative transformations and externalizing talk in a reflecting team consultation. *Qualitative Social Work,* 5(3), 313-332.

White, M. (2007). *Maps of narrative practice.* New York: W. W. Norton.

7
Single-session groups in healthcare: Two approaches to program evaluation

Barbara Muskat and Joanne Sulman

Abstract: In healthcare settings, single-session groups are a common modality owing to their significant benefits, both for participants and for the delivery of social work services. In these meetings, social group workers build a brief community for inclusion, connection, social support and the sharing of experience. Despite growing literature on evidence-based group work, there is a paucity of evaluation and research on single-session groups. This paper begins to address this gap by piloting an evaluation of group process in single-session groups. Quality assurance feedback from single-session groups in two hospitals provides preliminary evidence about whether and how single-session groups are helpful.

Keywords: social groupwork, single-session groups, evaluation, evidence-based practice

Introduction

Single-session group practice has been described as a source of significant benefits, both for participants and for the delivery of social work services (Ebenstein, 1999; Holmes-Garrett, 1990; Kosoff, 2003; Rotholz, 1985). These groups are a venue for the provision of information, connection, social support and the sharing of experience. They create a feeling of inclusion in a community of people who are "in the same boat" (Steinberg, 2004). Single-session groups can also be models of anti-oppressive practice based on social justice, social action, advocacy, community and diversity. As a strengths-based practice that utilizes purposeful activity and mutual aid, single-session groups are particularly useful in healthcare and can fulfill important needs for patients, families, staff and the organization.

Despite the growing literature on evidence-based groupwork (Macgowan, 2006, 2008), there is still little evaluation and research on single-session groups (Turnbull, Galinsky, Wilner, & Meglin, 1994). However, Steinberg (2010) noted that "when a group participant claims that mutual aid is taking place, the best possible evidence of its existence is manifest" (p.54). Adopting that perspective, this paper will describe the design and pilot of evaluations using participant feedback from single-session support groups for patients and families at two large urban teaching hospitals in Toronto, Canada. Both hospitals have previously employed a variety of member satisfaction methods that have consistently reported positive outcomes. However these methods have not specifically focused on evaluation of group process and mutual aid.

Literature review

The experience of living with medical conditions can be very difficult for patients and their families (Daste & Rose, 2005; Getzel, 2004; Webb, 2009). For patients, the experience of having an acute or chronic condition is generally painful and stress- inducing, with fear and worry about the present and the future. Families of patients commonly spend significant time caring and providing nurturance for their family member. Common to both patients and their families are experiences specific to the medical condition and the isolation that may accompany time spent in healthcare settings. These may include adjustment to the condition, financial pressures from missing work or medically-related costs, and limited accessible information about the condition and managing home-related duties (Ainbinder et al., 1998). Galinsky and Schopler (1995) detail the provision of social support through groups for persons in crisis, in life transitions, and for those living with chronic conditions. In healthcare settings, group support has been found to buffer the stress and isolation common for patients and their families (Getzel, 2004; Magen & Glajchen, 1999).

Social support and groupwork in healthcare settings

In recent years, changes in the healthcare system have made it more difficult for individuals in hospital and their families to connect with and to offer support to one another. These changes include infection control measures that limit interaction among patients, and lengths of stay that have decreased dramatically, resulting in rapid patient turnover. Those patients who remain in hospital tend to be critically ill, hooked to monitors and equipment, with family members carrying out more and more bedside care. An increasingly common approach to supporting patients and their families in today's healthcare settings is the use of single-session groups.

The basis for a model of single-session groups in health settings has been reported in the social work literature. Ebenstein (1999) described single-session groups as venues for bringing individuals together on a one-time basis to discuss concerns, express fears, share information and receive support. Block (1985) described these groups as 'open... by definition and by necessity" (p. 83). Kosoff (2003) added that these groups offer opportunities for development of mutual aid, and a place to share concerns and learn coping strategies. Steinberg (2004) succinctly stated that in these groups "the first meeting is also its last" (p. 193), requiring continual awareness by the worker and group members of the inevitable and quickly arising group termination. Block (1985) asserted that it is the role of the groupworker to provide a continuity of purpose from each single-session to the next, becoming the 'keeper of the group flame' (p. 95).

Mutual aid

Mutual aid has often been cited as a pivotal process in social work groups. Mutual aid refers to the helping system created in groups, where members and the leader work together to create multiple helping relationships (Gitterman, 2004; Schwartz, 1961; Shulman, 2006; Steinberg, 2004). In a mutual aid system members experience a common purpose, share common issues, develop bonds and collectively support and comfort one another in an effort to gain mastery over their common struggles. Shulman (1986, 2006) and Steinberg (2004) described nine processes that comprise a framework for mutual aid. These include 1) sharing data; 2) the dialectical process; 3) discussing taboo topics; 4) an 'all in the same boat' phenomenon; 5) mutual support; 6) mutual demand; 7) individual problem solving; 8) rehearsal; and 9) strength in numbers. These processes are seen as essential for members to overcome obstacles and frustrations, to support and confront one another and to deal with fears and apprehensions.

Steinberg (2004) argues that while it takes a "leap of faith" (p.194) to offer a meaningful experience in one session of a group, the potential for mutual aid is possible in single-session groups. She further asserts that single-session groups can

> give people an opportunity to see that others are in the same boat, to vent their frustrations, to share concerns and anxieties, to hear how others cope with problems or manage special situations or circumstances, and even to think about new ways of being and doing (p.195).

Referring to groups in healthcare, Glassman (1991) points to one of the unique features of the social work group that generates its healing qualities: the purposeful development of a democratic mutual aid system that enhances belonging and choice.

Creating community and free interaction

As in other groups, single-session groups contain the possibility of empowerment and creating community. This refers to a place that not only provides mutual support, motivation and practical help for members, but also gives them the opportunity to feel a sense of kinship with each other and to experience their strengths. As Breton (1994) notes, "mutual aid groups are ideal places for people to find and to learn to use their voices" (p. 32). Breton also encourages social groupworkers to create, engage and recognize community in their work (2010). Lang (2010) elaborated the power of purpose and free interaction: "Professional and member purposes are combined in a compound unlike that occurring in groups without a social worker" (p.84). She further stated that one of the essential elements of social groupwork practice was the "use of natural, nonsynthetic, spontaneous interaction processes" (p.122). For Lang, the groupwork context of free interaction becomes an authentic social reality, with "group experience as an analogic, nonlinear route to change" (p.122).

Groups and collectivities

Although we use the term *group* in this paper, single session practice that utilizes social groupwork skills takes place in collectivities rather than in small groups. Collectivity is a small social form consisting of a number of people gathered for a specific purpose, and has some of the features of fully-formed groups such as mutual aid, interaction, shared goals, and some sense of entity (Lang, 1986; Sulman, 1987; Sulman, Fletcher, Gayler, & Sokolsky, 1986). Not all collectivities are single-session groups. Some collectivities are formed owing to limitations in the client population that preclude autonomous functioning in a group, and others are the product of temporal or other limitations of the setting, and crisis or short-term practice (Sulman, 1987). In acute care, the rapid admission and discharge of patients often dictates the use of collectivity in order to deliver groupwork programs. In the collectivities referred to at sites in this paper (coffee hours or IBD drop-in groups), participants just "show up" or drop in. Collectivity can evolve over the course of several meetings, with members coming sporadically, as the presence of even one member with previous experience in the meeting seems to provide continuity (a peer co-leader is doubly helpful in this regard). Each group, however, is a unique single session, as there is usually a new constellation of unscreened members participating in each session. Because the term *collectivity* is meaningless to participants and colleagues, in practice we refer to single sessions as *groups*. In evaluating the utility of the single-sessions described in this paper, we looked for evidence of common group processes that occur in more fully-formed groups.

Evidence-based groupwork

Over the past decade social work has seen a growing focus on evidence-based practice (Pollio, 2006). Evidence-based practice demonstrates the value, quality, and effectiveness of service (Mace, 2006). It requires social workers to go beyond their practice judgment to assess the effectiveness of services offered and includes systematic collection and appraisal of evidence to see whether client results are achieved (Macgowan, 2006, 2008). While there has been growth in research about the effectiveness of group intervention (Muskat, Mishna, Farnia,

& Wiener, 2010; Ward, 2004) there has been very little written about the effectiveness of single-session groups. Block (1985) asserted that despite the increase in the use of these groups in hospital settings, there "remains ambivalence about their feasibility, effectiveness and appropriateness" (p. 96).

Turnbull, Galinsky, Wilner and Meglin (1994) examined outcomes in single-session groups for families of psychiatric patients. They studied family members' perceptions of information about illness and treatment, their ability to cope with family member's illness and hospitalization, and the amount of support received from the group and outside the hospital setting. Results showed overall effectiveness in all three areas.

Regehr and Hill (2001) used subjective measures and psychometric tools to evaluate individual outcomes of firefighters in single-session crisis debriefing groups with mixed results. Although individual outcomes were promising, group process outcomes were not addressed. Feigin, Cohen and Gilad (1998) collected feedback from participants in single-session groups for caregivers of elderly patients who were about to be discharged home. Feedback was collected at the end of each session and up to eight months after group participation. Early feedback indicated a better understanding of available services, decreased feelings of isolation, learning from other members and decreased initial anxiety. Importantly at 8 months after discharge, participants still recalled the sessions as helpful, stressing emphases on feelings of universality and normalization regarding the medical condition and related issues. Further they recalled feeling less isolation, less fearful and having increased knowledge. This resulted in a recommendation to continue offering these groups, due to their promise as an efficient approach for support to family members.

Evaluation of groupwork in healthcare calls for examination of both outcomes and member perceptions of group process in order to best understand what occurs in these groups (Magen & Glajchen, 1999). Given the very limited study of group outcome and process in single-session groups, the purpose of this paper is to examine the particular ways in which participants view the effectiveness or helpfulness of single-session groups. The paper will further explore whether elements of group process can be documented through evaluating this model of practice.

Project design

This pilot project examined qualitative data derived from quality assurance feedback in single-session support groups at two large acute-care teaching hospitals in Toronto, Canada. One of the hospitals is a pediatric hospital and the other is an adult facility. The questions posed were whether the groups were helpful and whether quality assurance feedback from participants was consistent with social groupwork practice theory noted in the literature.

Project background: Pediatric hospital

Support groups in the form of parent 'coffee hours' have been held for over ten years in a large urban pediatric hospital. Participants in the coffee hours are recruited from families whose children are patients on a specific unit and who may have similar medical conditions or experiences, such as recent surgery, gastrointestinal or cardiac conditions, organ transplantation and bone marrow transplantation. The groups, which are held in available meeting rooms on most inpatient units, generally operate once a week for about an hour and are facilitated by social workers. Groupworkers provide an open forum for discussion, written handouts which include relevant hospital and community-based resources, and coffee and snacks for participants. The groups have been designed to allow family members to meet one another; to share experiences, ideas and information; to give and receive empathic support, and to offer hope to one another (Winch & Christoph, 1988).

Project background: Adult hospital

In an adult acute care hospital in the same urban center, single-session groups with parents have been running for over two decades in the neonatal intensive care unit and for patients and families on the inflammatory bowel disease (IBD) service. In addition, the orthopedic oncology service has held single-session groups for the past ten years (Sulman et al., in press). These groups have similar purposes to the coffee hours in the pediatric hospital.

Methods

There are a number of challenges in carrying out an evaluation of a group session that lasts for only one to two hours and which many individuals attend only once. First, it is not practical for an evaluation to take more time than the intervention it is measuring. Moreover it is challenging to engage participants with limited available time in evaluation measures, and there is no established measure that has been used to examine outcome and process in single-session groups. Facilitators of the groups from both the pediatric and adult hospital settings had regularly collected verbal and written feedback from participants, and while the feedback was overwhelmingly positive, it has provided little information about what exactly made the groups effective for the participants. The authors therefore decided to gather feedback prospectively and to use groupwork practice theory to aid in the analysis.

Gathering quality assurance feedback in the pediatric setting

To address the challenges related to evaluation, group leaders in the pediatric hospital participated in a series of meetings to review the purpose of the coffee hour groups, the benefits to group attendees, and to develop a feasible approach to evaluation. It was important to the group leaders to find a way to collect feedback systematically that would allow members to openly share their own thoughts and words. The discussions informed the design of a short feedback form, which was granted approval for piloting by the hospital's quality management department. The form was comprised of three open questions:

*   Did you find this group to be helpful?
*   If so, how was it helpful?
*   If not, why was it not helpful?

    The form was distributed to all coffee hour participants from March-May, 2011. Forty (40) participants completed the forms. Participants included family members of pediatric in-patients in medical, surgical and cardiology units.

Gathering quality assurance feedback in the adult setting

Because feedback forms had yielded scant information, the workers in the IBD support groups decided to include "talking feedback" as part of purposeful endings. During March and April, 2011, at the end of each group session, the following questions were posed to a total of 25 participants in 3 group sessions:

• Did you find this group helpful? (If yes, why? If not, why not?)
• Were there other things that you would have liked to get from the group?

Responses from participants in both the pediatric and adult settings were collated, summarized and analyzed for repeating themes. The themes will be described, compared and contrasted with selected elements of practice theory found in the literature, particularly those that reflect mutual aid, and those that describe other social groupwork processes.

Analysis of themes from participant feedback

Mutual aid

Mutual aid, as noted above, is comprised of nine dynamic processes, including: sharing data, the dialectical process, discussing taboo topics, the 'all in the same boat' phenomenon, mutual support, mutual demand, individual problem solving, rehearsal and strength in numbers.

Sharing data

According to Steinberg (2004), the process of *sharing data* includes the group functioning as a "marketplace for the exchange of information and ideas" (p.249), in which members see one another as sources of information. Not only does the group provide concrete information, it helps members make meaning of that information.

In the pediatric coffee hours, learning new information was frequently cited as a valuable experience. Comments such as "more information and resources to help us through the experience at the hospital", and "information about tax deduction, fees, parking and workouts and spas" underscore the importance of a having a place where parents can get basic information to help them navigate the unfamiliar and stressful environment of a hospital. Sharing data was also described as important in the adult groups: "I found out that communication is the key to intimate relationships whether people have an illness or not".

Dialectic process

The dialectic process allows for discussion of the pros and cons of the multiple perspectives regarding a topic (Cicchetti, 2011). Although this theme did not emerge verbatim, it can be inferred from comments that spoke of the importance of relating to and connecting with others who shared similar experiences but differing perspectives owing to their unique circumstances.

> *It was important to meet other parents, hear their stories and learn their strategies… It's encouraging when people get something to take away from the group, and weird how small things can make such a difference…I was surprised by the school discrimination [against IBD] - I'm going to find out what kind of law that it falls under.*

All in the same boat

The theme of "all in the same boat" was evident in much of the participant feedback. Members' comments illustrated the power that comes from realizing that others share aspects of one's troubling experiences.

> *It's people's experience – you're not alone, not the only one…I've never talked to anybody else with my condition – it's awesome… Hearing the*

stories of the other parents was helpful...Lets you talk with other parents, making you realize you're not always worst off, or the only one going through the same thing.

Discussing taboos

Taboo topics are subjects that people feel uncomfortable talking about, or that carry a perceived stigma. This important theme was repeatedly reflected in the feedback from group participants. Examples include: "Just to talk about it – to *be able* to talk about it!" and "None of my friends know what it's like to have a sick child", and "I feel like I can be 100% honest here".

Coping strategies

In addition to offering a sense of common experience, group participation assisted members to learn how other participants coped with problems. From feedback at both sites, group members described that they learned new strategies for coping, were able to hear others' stories, and to learn what to do the next time they encountered similar obstacles. One participant noted: "Other people's experience triggers things you haven't thought of – you can take it home and think about it".

Mutual support

Mutual support has been characterized by Steinberg as "a direct here-and-now forum for mutual aid" (2004, p.194). The term *mutual support* describes interactions reflecting the affective components of mutual aid and the offering of support to one another. Participants gave feedback about this helping feature.

There was another mother like me - we both worry about our daughters - we can support and understand each other...Talking to other parents was helpful and made me feel better... I received emotional and psychological support from the group.

Hope, comfort and encouragement

In addition to describing mutual support experienced in the group, members gave more specific feedback about feelings of hope, comfort and encouragement that they derived from the groups.

> *It gives you hope–people can get into relationships [even though they have this illness]...I'm encouraged by others' responses...There's comfort in hearing others' stories...I've never actually talked to another person with this illness face-to-face: it's comforting.*

Individual problem solving

One purpose of offering coffee hours or support groups is that the experience will resonate and assist participants to find solutions to the difficult challenges they face. Group participants commented on new approaches to problem solving they discovered in the groups.

The group gave me insight and knowledge about new information that was helpful to me...It introduced a few items that I wasn't aware of before travelling here...I was relieved to hear people [with IBD] talk about their successful pregnancies...I feel reassured - I'm not always the worst off.

Other dynamics of mutual aid

While there was less feedback related to other dynamics of mutual aid that are mentioned in the literature, there was some evidence of their presence. Participants stated that they learned better ways to talk to doctors and other staff (*rehearsal*). *Mutual demand* was in evidence in the member-to-member interactions that workers observed, and also from people openly expressing that they would have liked to hear more from each other about specific topics.

Additional social groupwork processes

Free interaction

The experience of free interaction that allows people to know each other (Lang, 2010) was described as a core attribute of the helping process in the groups.

> *It's hearing about people's experiences in common...Learning from other members in the group...Hearing about the resources and also simply listening and talking...*

Power of purpose

Establishing the purpose of a group, particularly in single-session groups, has been described as key to their success (Block, 1985). While mutual aid can occur in a quick encounter along a hospital corridor, single-session groups offer more than mutual aid. They have a purpose and a sense of people going somewhere together.

> *This group is important–it's a support network of people who understand... The group shows the importance of relating to and connecting with others who share similar experiences...The group was helpful in that it gave me more thorough knowledge of things I already knew - also it gave me insight and knowledge about new information that was helpful to me...I actually met other parents.*

Creating community

Through the analysis of the participant feedback, similar comments related to the themes of *belonging* and *strength in numbers* were collapsed into the single theme, *creating community*. Group members noted the importance of relating to and connecting with others who shared similar experiences. They also commented on the experience of participating in a support network which not only reflected community but also a sense of belonging and strength in numbers, or the *strength in us* (Breton 2004): "This group is important–it's a support network of people who understand"; and "the group showed the importance of relating to and connecting with others who share similar experiences".

Focus on strengths

Social work groups are assumed to be strengths-based approaches to practice. Participants in the single-session groups spoke of appreciating not being defined by their illness or problem: "I don't have to think of myself as 'damaged goods' – I have lots of other parts of me. I'm not just my illness". Participants talked about the importance of learning from the wisdom of other members: "I was helped by others' experience", and the inherent fun in groups, "just laughing and talking about every day life".

Group process: Primary force for change

Middleman and Wood (1990) refer to the role of the group process itself as a primary force responsible for individual and collective change. Shulman (1986) characterizes mutual aid as a process and a result. These authors illuminate the critical importance of group process. Feedback from participants in the single-session groups supports the importance of group process. Although feedback did not include specific comments about group process *per se*, members indicated that engaging with others in group was meaningful, helpful and productive: "Learning from other members; the importance of relating to and connecting with others who share similar experiences; hearing the stories of the other parents was helpful; the group was a chance to express our concerns and share information".

Limitations reported by participants

In addition to the many positive comments received from participants, feedback also indicated a desire for more time in the group, additional participants, more frequent group meetings and wanting opportunities to take the content further: "I wish we had more time to talk about communication". The single session often left participants "wanting more".

Discussion

The feedback described above indicates that participants experienced benefits from the groups, that the groups were useful in addressing needs related to healthcare experiences and that group processes occurred that are similar to those that take place in all social work groups.

The concept of mutual aid has been described as a basic tenet within social groupwork theory (Gitterman, 2004; Schwartz, 1961; Shulman, 2006; Steinberg, 2004). Shulman (2006) characterizes mutual aid as a process and a result: As a process, mutual aid is what group members do together to be helpful; as a result it is what group members experience from having interacted with others in a particular way. Steinberg (2004) asserts that single-session groups can at least offer members 'a taste' of mutual aid, or function in a way that is similar to the beginning stage of a longer-term mutual aid-based group. However, feedback from participants noted in this paper indicates that many dynamics of mutual aid were apparent to them in the groups. The dynamics described included sharing data, the dialectic process, discussing taboos, 'all in the same boat', mutual support, mutual demand, individual problem solving, rehearsal, and strength in numbers.

From the worker perspective, Middleman and Wood (1990) described essential criteria for social work process in any group: the presence of a worker who helps members become a system of mutual aid, and a worker who understands that the group process itself is a powerful force for individual and collective change. Lang (1979, 2010) described the importance of free interaction and the power of purpose that shape a social work group. Fostering a sense of community has also been posited as an essential feature of social work with groups (Breton, 2010). Finally a focus on strengths has been described as a hallmark of social groupwork practice (Lee, 1993; Pottick, 1989).

Despite the brief amount of time spent in a single-session group, the features of establishment of purpose, enhancement of free and open interaction, honoring group members as mutual helpers, focusing on strengths and developing a sense of belonging to a group community were both possible and experienced as beneficial.

Worker role in single-session groups

How do groupworkers create a venue for powerful mutual aid to occur in a single session? As in collectivity and in any group in its beginning phases, the worker in single sessions is often more active. Primary tasks are to foster connection, belonging and the development of mutual aid. In order for mutual aid to occur, the groupworker must quickly engage members, establish the group's purpose, develop trust among group members, respect that some members will likely not share experiences, and hold the group to purpose while responding to members' needs (Steinberg, 2004).

Even though single-session groups were described by Steinberg (2004) as resembling the beginning phases of groups, all groups including single-session groups have beginnings, middles and endings. Beginnings typically include introductions, a statement of purpose for the group, a description of what to expect, establishment of confidentiality, and a brief statement by participants of why they came to the group. Workers give permission for members to engage, and provide safety to express feelings in order to encourage group members to interact authentically (Sulman et al., in press). Middles work on issues related to purpose, employing discussion and/or a program piece such as menu planning with a dietitian, role play about speaking with medical staff or going home with a baby from the neonatal intensive care unit. Endings sum up salient themes, check for unresolved issues, elicit feedback, and ensure that everyone feels safe to leave the group. Similar to phases of group development (Garland, Jones & Kolodny, 1978; Schiller, 2007), every session's beginning, middle and ending are opportunities for mutual aid, free interaction and the expression of group purpose.

Nevertheless, there are inherent limitations to single-session groups. These groups can never become autonomous or reap the benefits of group membership that a fully developed social work group can offer. Even the simplest social action initiative requires extensive worker mediation. At best, the single-session format group can evolve into a very loose collectivity with a core membership derived from members attending during subsequent hospital admissions or returning as out-patients.

Limitations of this program evaluation

The purpose of this program evaluation was to explore in a preliminary way whether or not *social groupwork* was happening in the single sessions that staff were facilitating. The data are not from research studies and are not generalizable. Since they were program evaluations only, the projects were not submitted for research ethics review, and no demographic or other identifying information was gathered. The number of participants providing feedback in this project was small (a total of 65 participants in the two hospital settings).

Our data suggest that although single-session groups can reflect some of the features of fully-formed groups, there is a need for a more complete exploration of the benefits and short-comings of single-session groups in healthcare settings.

Conclusion

This paper discusses an evaluation of single-session groups in two acute care hospital settings. Responding to open-ended questions, participants used their words and ideas to describe group outcomes. The feedback revealed that despite the limitations of the format, single-session group members are pleased with their experiences. Further, group members described experiences that reflected dynamics of mutual aid and other group processes that underlie individual and collective change. The feedback is relevant since the themes match characteristics that social groupworkers hope to find in all social work groups.

Future directions for evaluation of single-session groups include moving from program evaluation to a full research project. Research questions should include: (1) If single-session groups help, how exactly do they help? (2) What have groupworkers done to create the groundwork for mutual aid and other group processes? (3) How can this be measured? (4) And what can members tell us about the longer-term impact of single-session groups for them? From the feedback received from participants in coffee hours and drop-in groups, we suggest that the single-session format group is worth further exploration as a purposeful addition to groupwork methodology.

References

Ainbinder, J., Blanchard, L.W., Singer, G.H.S., Sullivan, M.E., Powers, L.K., Marquis, J.G., Santelli, B., & the Consortium to Evaluate Parent to Parent. (1998). A qualitative study of parent to parent support for parents of children with special needs. *Journal of Pediatric Psychology, 23*(2), 99-109.

Block, L.R. (1985). On the potentiality and limits of time: The single-session group and the cancer patient. *Social Work with Groups, 8*(2), 81-99.

Breton, M. (1994). On the meaning of empowerment and empowerment-oriented social work practice. *Social Work with Groups, 17*(3), 23-37.

Breton, M. (2004). An empowerment perspective. In C. Garvin, L. Gutierrez, & M. Galinsky (Eds.), *Handbook of Social Work with Groups* (pp. 58-75). New York, NY: Guilford Press.

Breton, M. (2010, October). *Solidarity and groupwork responsibility to connect groups to communities.* Paper presented at The Toronto Region Groupworkers Network: A Groupwork Practice Showcase.

Daste, B.M., & Rose, S.R. (2005). Groupwork with cancer patients. In G.L. Greif & P. H. Ephross, (Eds.), *Groupwork with Populations at Risk, 2nd Edition* (pp. 15-30). New York, NY: Oxford University Press.

Cicchetti, A. (2011). *Mutual aid processes: Specific processes,* Retrieved from www.mutualaidbasedgroupwork.com/groupworktheory

Ebenstein, H. (1999). Single-session groups: Issues for social workers. *Social Work with Groups, 21*(1-2), 49-60.

Feigin, R., Cohen, I., & Gilad, M. (1998). The use of single-group sessions in discharge planning. *Social Work in Healthcare, 2*(3), 19-38.

Garland, J.A., Jones, H.E., & Kolodny, R.L. (1978). A model for stages of development in social work groups. In S. Bernstein (Ed.), *Explorations in Groupwork* (pp.12-53). Hebron, CT: Practitioners Press.

Galinsky, M. J., & Schopler, J. H. (1995). *Support groups: Current perspectives on theory and practice.* Binghamton, NY: The Haworth Press.

Getzel, G. (2004). Groups in physical and mental health. In C.D. Garvin, L. M. Gutierrez, & M. J. Galinsky (Eds.), *Handbook of Social Work with Groups* (pp. 195-211). New York, NY: Guilford Press.

Gitterman, A. (2004). The mutual aid model. In C.D. Garvin, L. M. Gutierrez, & M. J. Galinsky (Eds.), *Handbook of Social Work with Groups* (pp. 93-110), New York, NY: Guilford Press.

Glassman, U. (1991). The social work group and its distinct healing qualities in the healthcare setting. *Health and Social Work, 16*(3), 203-12.

Holmes-Garrett, C. (1990). The crisis of the forgotten family: A single-session group in the ICU waiting room. *Social Work with Groups, 12*(4), 141-157.

Kosoff, S. (2003). Single-session groups: Applications and areas of expertise. *Social Work with Groups, 26*(1), 29-45.

Lang, N. C. (1979). Some defining characteristics of the social work group: Unique social form. In S.L. Abels & P. Abels (Eds.), *Social Work with Groups: Proceedings of the 1979 symposium on Social Work with Groups* (pp. 18-50). Louisville, KY: Committee for the Advancement of Social Work with Groups.

Lang, N. C. (1986). Social work practice in small social forms: Identifying collectivity. *Social Work with Groups, 9*(4), 7-32.

Lang, N.C. (2010). *Groupwork Practice to Advance Social Competence.* New York: Columbia University Press.

Lee, J.A.B. (1993). Jane Addams in Boston: Intersecting time and space. *Social Work with Groups, 15*(2), 7–21.

Mace, C. (2006). Setting the world on wheels: Some clinical challenges of evidence-based practice. *Group Analysis, 39*(3), 304–320.

Macgowan, M. J. (2006). Evidence-based groupwork: A framework for advancing best practice. *Journal of Evidence-Based Social Work, 3*(1), 1-21.

Macgowan, M. J. (2008). A *Guide to Evidence-Based Groupwork.* New York: Oxford University Press.

Magen, R., & Glajchen, M. (1999). Cancer support groups: Client outcome and the context of group process. *Research on Social Work Practice, 9*(5), 541-554

Middleman, R. R., & Goldberg Wood, G. (1990). From social groupwork to social work with groups. *Social Work with Groups, 13*(3), 3-20.

Muskat, B., Mishna, F., Farnia, F., & Wiener, J. (2010). We may not like it but we guess we have to do it: Bringing agency-based staff on board with evidence-based groupwork. *Social Work with Groups, 33*(2), 229-247.

Pollio, D. E. (2006). The art of evidence-based practice. *Research on Social Work Practice, 16*(2), 224–232.

Pottick, K. J. (1989). Jane Addams revisited. *Social Work with Groups, 11*(4), 11- 26.

Regehr, C. & Hill, J. (2001). Evaluating the efficacy of crisis debriefing groups, *Social Work with Groups, 23*(3), 69-79.

Rotholz, T. (1985). The single-session group: An innovative approach to the waiting room. *Social Work with Groups, 8*(2), 143-146.

Schiller, L.Y. (2007). Not for women only: Applying the relational model of group development with vulnerable populations. *Social Work with Groups, 30*(2), 11-26.

Schwartz, W. (1961). The social worker in the group. In B. Saunders (Ed.), *New perspectives on services to groups: Theory, organization, practice,* (pp.7-29). New York, NY: NASW.

Shulman, L. (1986). The dynamics of mutual aid. In A. Gitterman and L. Shulman (Eds.), *The legacy of William Schwartz: Group practice as shared interaction* (51-60). New York, NY: Haworth Press.

Shulman, L. (2006). *The skills of helping: Individuals, families, groups, and communities* (5th ed.). Belmont, CA: Thompson.

Steinberg, D. M. (2004). *Mutual aid approach to working with groups* (2nd ed.). Binghamton, NY: Haworth Press.

Steinberg, D.M. (2010). Mutual aid: A contribution to best practice social work. *Social Work with Groups, 33*(1), 53-68.

Sulman, J., Fletcher, J., Gayler, C., & Sokolsky, A. (1986). A collectivity of impaired elderly in an acute care hospital: Practice and research. *Social Work with Groups, 9* (4), 45-58.

Sulman, J. (1987). The worker's role in collectivity. In N. C. Lang & J. Sulman (Eds.), *Collectivity in social groupwork* (pp. 59-67). New York, NY: Haworth Press.

Sulman, J., Verhaeghe, L., Coulthard, C., MacDonell, K., Oke, A., Sokolsky, A. W., Woodhead, T., & Worrod, S. (In press). Groupwork at the heart of hospital social work practice: Creating inclusion and solidarity in the acute care environment. *Proceedings of 32nd International Symposium for the Advancement of Social Work with Groups.* London: Whiting & Birch.

Turnbull, J.E., Galinsky, M.J., Wilner, M.E., & Meglin, D.E. (1994). Designing research to meet service needs: An evaluation of single-session groups for families of psychiatric inpatients. *Research on Social Work Practice, 4*(2), 192-207.

Ward, D. E. (2004). The evidence mounts: Groupwork is effective. *Journal for Specialists in Groupwork, 29*(2), 155–157.

Webb, N.B. (Ed.). (2009). Helping *children and adolescents with chronic and serious medical conditions: A strengths-based approach.* Hoboken, N.J.: Wiley.

Winch, A.E., & Christoph, J.M. (1988). Parent-to-parent links: Building networks for parents of hospitalized children. *CHC, 17*(2), 93-97.

8
Self-hypnosis groups for teaching relaxation and dealing with stress

Kay Goler Levin

Abstract: *By practicing relaxation and self-hypnosis, individuals dealing with stress can be helped to cope. A group format can be a very useful vehicle for teaching stress reduction skills. This workshop presented how through the use of a group modality, relaxation and self- hypnosis can be taught and practiced. The group process facilitates teaching self-hypnosis. A synergy is created between group dynamics and self-hypnosis content that supports and intensifies the hypnosis, while the group experience of trust and support facilitates and expands capacity for processing within the group. People learn better with people that they trust and a supportive group is an especially effective way to build that trust.*

Keywords: hypnosis, groups, stress reduction, relaxation

Introduction

I first offered to teach self-hypnosis to cancer survivors at Gilda's Club, in Chicago. Being a seasoned groupworker, I decided to utilize a groupwork approach. The interactions among the individuals in the group enriched the teaching and experiencing of self-hypnosis. I was able to replicate this group experience with anxious first year medical students. The focus for the medical students was to more effectively deal with the stressors of medical school.

Overview of paper and workshop

I found that there is a synergy between the principles of self-hypnosis and group work, which is explored in the paper. "Learning self-hypnosis principles demystifies hypnosis and empowers the patient," (Rostafinski, 2007). Learning within a group, can offer more solutions and suggestions, as well as, present some problems. Those challenges and benefits will be discussed, along with some of the myths, expectations and fears that people bring to the idea of hypnosis. Fears often stop people from learning more about hypnosis.

Hypnosis is defined as a "state of inner absorption, concentration and focused attention. It is like using a magnifying glass to focus the rays of the sun and make them more powerful. Similarly when our minds are concentrated and focused, we are able to use our minds more powerfully. Because hypnosis allows people to use more of their potential, learning self-hypnosis is the ultimate act of self–control" (American Society of Clinical Hypnosis [ASCH] general information statement). This is in contrast to one of the most common myths, that one loses control when hypnotized.

Teaching self-hypnosis in a group of cancer survivors at Gilda's Club or to graduate medical students presents opportunities to not only teach the principles of self-hypnosis, but also to utilize group work principles. The interaction of self-hypnosis and group work creates new and interesting ways for people to reformulate or reframe issues, and consequently identify new solutions. This effectively combines self-hypnosis and group therapy, by using the group experience to help discuss and process new solutions to existing problems (Spiegel and Spiegel, 2004; Yalom, 2005). This approach allows the group members to focus on looking at many answers to a problem, as well as, exploring their individual experiences with hypnosis.

Hypnosis: Definitions and myths

The word "hypnosis" originates from the Greek word "hypnos" which means sleep. The term was coined by James Braid (1786-1860); however, today we know hypnosis is not a form of sleep. Contrary to sleep, current brain scans (EEGs) of individuals who are hypnotized and in a trance state show them to "become more alert and awake than usual and in a very focused state of mind. Sleep and a trance state share a relative diminution of peripheral awareness, but when one is asleep, focal awareness is dissolved, whereas in the trance state it is intensified" (Spiegel & Spiegel, 2004). The EEGs of hypnotized individuals show a high incidence of alpha activity during the trance state. "Alpha activity is most often described as the noise that the brain makes when it is alert and resting and is inconsistent with EEG patterns observed during sleep" (London et al. 1969).

In reviewing the literature on hypnosis, one finds many definitions. Hypnosis can be understood as an altered state of consciousness, according to CC Tart (1969) who believed that human beings are capable of shifting from one state of consciousness to another in any given 24 hour period. He believed that this was how healthy human beings went through life and that the experience was so natural to us that we would not notice it.

People often fear that being hypnotized will make them lose control, surrender their will and result in being dominated, but a hypnotic state is not the same thing as gullibility or weakness. Many people base their assumptions about hypnotism on stage acts but fail to take into account that stage hypnotists screen their volunteers to select those who are cooperative, with possible exhibitionist tendencies, as well as responsiveness to hypnosis. Stage acts help create a myth about hypnosis which discourages people from seeking legitimate hypnotherapy (ASCH information statement).

Those fears are often heard when people are reticent to think about self-hypnosis. What is often expressed is that I don't want to lose control, and I'm afraid of looking ridiculous, or that you'll make me act ridiculous, in ways that I wouldn't otherwise. And in stage acts that is often what has happened. These examples are usually the first discussed with patients or groups. Another fear that often makes people uncomfortable about hypnosis is the fear that "people lose consciousness and have amnesia. A small percentage of subjects who go into very deep levels of trance will fit this stereotype and have spontaneous amnesia. The majority of people remember everything that occurs in hypnosis. This is beneficial, because the most of what we want to accomplish in hypnosis may be done in a medium depth trance, where people tend to remember everything" (ASCH statement).

The difference between hypnosis used as entertainment, and without the ethics and values of the medical hypnotherapist and hypnosis as a part of a therapeutic alliance with the group member's full agreement is that "there is an alliance, and nothing is done without the client's permission. The patient is not under the control of the hypnotist. Hypnosis is not something imposed on people, but something they do for themselves. A hypnotist simply serves as a facilitator to guide them" (ASCH statement). "All hypnosis is self-hypnosis" (Rostafinski, 2007). The therapist works with the client, and the client is told from the beginning that they will do nothing that they don't want to do, that they have the ability to come out of the trance whenever they wish to. That nothing is or should be done without the permission of the patient, in fact most hypnotic suggestions are made as questions or suggestions. A trained hypnotherapist will only work with someone with their permission. That relationship and those expectations should be discussed and agreed upon from the beginning.

Myths and misconceptions

Some of the most common myths are: "Hypnosis is created in the subject by the power of the hypnotist. Hypnosis only occurs when induced by the hypnotist. Only persons of weak character can be hypnotized. People can become 'stuck' in a trance. Hypnosis is a form of therapy" (Torem, 1992). These myths often inhibit people from taking part in hypnosis. People are often afraid that the hypnotherapist will turn them into a chicken or make them run around acting silly or do something to embarrass themselves.

It is extremely helpful when people realize that the power to hypnotize lies within themselves. The process of teaching self-hypnosis can help to demystify it and can be empowering to the individual. The use of group process can help individuals to share their understanding, because

> Hypnosis allows us to more fully secure and focus the patient's attention on ideas and motivations. It also appears that hypnosis facilitates the more rapid evolution of a relaxed and trusting therapeutic relationship. Self-hypnosis allows patients to be more active in the therapeutic process and to utilize their innate capacity for cognitive control, giving a greater sense of personal involvement and mastery. (Hammond, 1998).

Indicators or contra-indicators

Offering self-hypnosis in a group affords a number of new and interesting possibilities. Some are good and some present challenges for the group worker. Some issues need special care when dealing with them in groups, and require special care when preparing group members. One must evaluate the following: Who is in the group, what are their issues, and, what is the level of their mental health? The other aspect that has great influence on the group interactions is the cohesion of the group, what are the common concerns of the group members? (In the Gilda's groups, there is the shared experience of dealing with cancer, and in the medical school groups, they had been together as a group for the school year). These issues influence the process and the discussions both before and after the hypnosis, and add a great deal to the experience.

The group worker needs not only to be skilled at hypnosis, but a skilled group worker as well. Group work skill plays an important part in what the group members are able to take away from the experience of the trance and what is achieved then, and what issues are looked at and processed both before and after the trance experience. The group discussions before the experience offer a chance to share problems and possibly brainstorm a range of solutions. Fears and expectations about the experience of hypnosis are also discussed. The group discussions after the self-hypnosis offer a chance to share what comes up and to debrief. One of the interesting reactions that has come up a few times now, is that when individuals were to go to their safe and desired place to retreat, instead of their own place, the person decided to visit someone else's place and explore that . The sharing seems to take place on many levels!

There is also a pre-test that is used to determine any underlying issues and to assess the individual's desire and hypnotizability. The group worker needs to have developed a relationship of trust with individual members, and ideally, the group members should have met for a while, so that they know and trust each other. Teaching self- hypnosis in a group is an activity for the middle or ending stages of a group. An exception may be groups with similar experiences, such as cancer-survivor groups, where mutual problems and fears will foster that cohesion a little faster. Ironically, some of this same awareness and feeling that 'we're all in the same boat' can be attributed to the first year medical students in a rigorous graduate program! What comes up are the uniquely individual experiences and triggers that are experienced individually, but in a group of trust, what can be observed then is the best of mutual- aid in a group as group members share experiences and solutions.

Self-hypnosis: What, why, and how

When I led a group workshop in order to teach self-hypnosis at Gilda's Club, my goal was to teach participants some methods of self-hypnosis to help them better get through the problems associated with cancer treatment: nausea from chemo, pain management, relaxation, or to get back to sleep when you awaken at 3 o'clock in the morning or when you can't get to sleep at all. The goal with the medical students was to help them relax and manage the various demands placed on them. This was offered at the end of the first year of medical school, after content on professionalism, ethics and decision- making in medicine, impaired physicians, and complementary medicine. The Gilda's workshops covered: What hypnosis is, What hypnosis isn't Myths and misconceptions, What hypnosis is good for, Assessment-why you might want to learn self-hypnosis, principles and process of self-hypnosis, the actual practice and trance induction, and follow-up discussion.

What hypnosis is has been discussed above. Some additional ideas presented included: Hypnosis is a phenomenon characterized by a state of attentive, receptive concentration containing three concurrent features of varying degrees: dissociation, absorption and suggestibility, all three of which need to be present (Spiegel & Spiegel, 2004). "Hypnosis is a procedure during which changes are suggested in sensations, perceptions, thought, feeling or behavior" (APA statement).

We believe hypnosis is facilitative because it allows patients to be more active in the therapeutic process and to utilize their innate capacity for cognitive control, giving a greater sense of personal involvement and mastery. We basically do three things in hypnosis: 1) Encourage the use of imagination – mental imagery is very powerful, especially in a focused state of attention (rather than using will power, hypnosis uses the power of imagination – the mind is capable of using imagery, even when only symbolic to assist in bringing about what we imagine). 2) Present ideas or suggestions to the patient in a state of concentrated attention, ideas that are compatible with the person's desires seem to have a more powerful effect on the mind. And 3) Finally hypnosis may be used for unconscious exploration, sometimes there may be underlying dynamics, motivations, or unresolved feelings about past events that may be influencing us (Hammond, 1998).

Many of these ideas can be discussed in the group beforehand, as group members share some of their goals for hypnosis, and discuss imagery that has special importance to each individual. One of the interesting things that often happen is that: at the beginning of the group we go around the group, and everyone is asked their favorite place to go. They share some memories of this place that is special to them. This provides a supportive group experience before they embark on the trance part of the group. And as I mentioned previously, this discussion and explanation about individual favorite places, often makes such an impression on individual group members that at the end of the group when they share their experiences we often find that they have visited another group member's special place.

What hypnosis isn't —or shouldn't be- is coercive: you don't lose control, surrender your will to another, and you will NOT be dominated by another. You don't lose consciousness, The therapist DOES NOT do this to you, rather you do this with the therapist, for reasons that you should agree to beforehand, for purposes that you desire and agree to! That should be explained to you at the beginning of every session, and the therapist should have the credentials and training from one of the professional hypnotherapy societies. Hypnotherapy is not meditation- and you can come out of the trance anytime you want to-and you can't be made to do anything that you don't want to, or wouldn't agree to while not in a trance.

As mentioned previously the synergy between teaching self-hypnosis and group process amplifies the power of both modalities. Experiencing hypnosis in a group often helps the individual to feel safer and more comfortable with the experience. Processing the experience within that group afterwards brings the opportunity for more observations and discussion about individual experiences with a chance for group support, acceptance and normalization of the variety of experiences.

References

American Psychological Association (www.apa.oirg/topics/hypnosis)

American Society of Clinical Hypnosis (www.asch.net)

Hammond, D.C. (Ed., 1990). *Handbook of hypnotic suggestions and metaphors.* New York: W.W. Norton & Company.

Highland, E.R. & Hildegard, J .R. (1994). *Hypnosis in the relief of pain.* New York: Brunner/Mazel.

Jensen, M. P., Barber, M., Hanley, M.A., Engel, J. M., Barber, J, Cardenas, D.D. et al. (2008). Long-term outcome of hypnotic analgesia treatment for chronic pain in persons with disabilities. *International Journal of Clinical and Experimental Hypnosis, 56,* 157-170.

Jensen, M. P. & Patterson, D. R. (2006). Hypnotic treatment of chronic pain, *Journal of Behavioral Medicine, 29,* 95-124.

London, P, Hart, J.T, et al. (1969). EEG, alpha rhythms and susceptibility to hypnosis. *Nature, 219,* 71-72.

Rostafinski, T.J., (2007), Third Benjamin Schwartz, M.D., Memorial workshop in medical hypnosis. Loyola University Medical Center, Chicago, Illinois.

Spiegel, D. & Bloom, J.R., (1983). Group therapy and hypnosis reduce metastatic breast carcinoma pain. *Psychosomatic Medicine. 45*(4), 333-339.

Spiegel, H. & Spiegel, D. (2004). *Trance and treatment: clinical uses of hypnosis, second edition.* Washington, D.C.: American Psychiatric Publishing Inc.

Tart. C.C. (Ed., 1969) *Altered states of consciousness.* Garden City, N.Y: Springer

Torem, M.S., (1992). Hypnosis: Lingering Myths and Established Facts. *Psychiatric Medicine, 10(1),* 1-11.

Yalom, I.D. (2005). *The theory and practice of group psychotherapy, 5th Edition,* New York: Basic Books.

9
A men's support group: An adjunct for men in psychotherapy

Ernest M. Gunderson

Abstract: This article describes a qualitative study of 11 men who had participated regularly and concurrently in individual psychotherapy and a men's support group. It was discovered that a men's support group and psychotherapy reinforce each other and create a synergistic learning environment for men in search of personal growth and emotional support. The participants expressed strong appreciation toward their men's support groups for providing emotional support and peer feedback on a variety of issues. The study provides useful information for therapists, social work clinicians and group workers who are treating male clients.

Keywords: *men's support group, psychotherapy*

Introduction

Studies have shown that men have more propensity than women for social isolation, and men are less likely to seek help for emotional problems (Brooks, 1998; Cochran, 2001; Levant, 1995; Pollack, 2001; Reddin & Sonn, 2003).). Evidence of this can be seen in the high suicide rates for men. According to the National Institute of Mental Health's (NIMH, 2009) statistics, men commit suicide at a rate four times greater than women. Isolation and depression were found to be among the highest risk factors.

Although peer-led or self-help support groups are not a substitute for group therapy or psychotherapy (Miller, 1998; Williams & Myer, 1992), several studies have highlighted the potential of these support groups as an intervention for isolation and depression (Kurtz & Powell, 1987; Reddin & Sonn, 2003; Richard, 2000; Sternbach, 1990). Little is known, however, about the potential synergies for men who participate concurrently in both psychotherapy and a men's support group which is the subject of this paper.

Review of literature

A review of existing literature turned up only one study on the effect of men's support group involvement on traditional psychotherapy. Williams and Myer (1992) did a case study on one therapy client who agreed to attend a men's retreat. Upon his return, the client showed a marked improvement in his willingness to express his emotions and to self-disclose in therapy. Although the Williams and Myer study reveals a potentially positive effect of men's group participation on psychotherapy, it was only one case, and it did not involve an on-going men's support group. More research is needed to determine the effect on a man's psychotherapy owing to his participation in a men's support group.

Conceptualizing a men's support group

Most ongoing men's support groups are peer-led or leaderless groups (Miller, 1998). The term *peer-led* refers to self-help groups that have no on-going appointed facilitator. This does not mean peer-led groups have no leadership or facilitation, for members of these groups often take turns facilitating the meetings (Kauth, 1992; Liebman, 1991; Reddin & Sonn, 2003). In peer-led groups such as Alcoholics Anonymous (AA) and other 12-step groups, Miller explains that leadership responsibility is rotated among experienced members who guide the process and uphold the rules. One advantage of the peer-led group is the minimal cost of operation (Kurtz and Powell, 1987; Miller, 1998).

Another advantage in leaderless or peer-led groups is the balance in leadership authority, where decisions are made by consensus (Liebman, 1991). Keen (1991) uses the term *spiritual democracy* to describe the equity of authority possible in a leaderless group. Yalom (1995), however, warned that leaderless groups must be cohesive and have well established norms to be effective. He valued leaderless group meetings and required his therapy groups to meet alone every third time. In these leaderless meetings, Yalom believed his clients would develop autonomy, responsibility, and a more natural group dynamic in which important issues and behaviors would arise, which did not always occur in his presence.

Not the same as counseling or group therapy

Although a peer-led men's support group provides growth opportunities and social support for its members, it is not group therapy nor is it a substitute for counseling (Miller, 1998; Williams & Myer, 1992). According to Miller, men's support groups are sometimes led by a therapist, either in a volunteer capacity or professional capacity, but the support group still follows a different format than group psychotherapy. The support group can be therapeutic, Miller points out, but that does not make it therapy. In group therapy it is the therapist's role to psychoanalyze and intervene with various educational or therapeutic inputs, which distinguishes it from a support group (Comstock & Mohamoud, 1990; Keen, 1991; Miller, 1998; Yalom, 1995). Clinicians who lead group therapy are more prepared to deal with members who act out in a disruptive way, with members who present symptoms of a serious mental illness, or with members who might require intervention for illegal activities or behavior (Schopler & Galinsky, 1995; Yalom, 2005).

Closed versus open groups

Closed men's support groups generally meet weekly or biweekly, have a fixed membership of five to ten men, often meet in each other's homes, require a commitment to attend regularly, and generally admit new members only when an existing member departs (Barton, 2000; Miller, 1998). The main advantage of the closed group is the level of intimacy, safety, and deep sharing, which is more achievable when group members are able to get better acquainted and develop trust and respect (Barton, 2000; Kauth, 1992; Keen, 1991).

Open men's support groups generally meet weekly, are open to any man who wants to participate, and have a fixed location and time schedule (Barton, 2000; Miller, 1998). Because attendance is optional, the number of participants can be highly variable, perhaps three or four attendees one week and nine or ten (often many more) the next week (Liebman,1991). Miller emphasizes the advantage of greater diversity in open groups. Open groups are available to any man in need of support because they are generally advertised and open to the public (Barton, 2000; Kauth, 1992).

Men in psychotherapy

Men are generally more resistant than women to entering psychotherapy; in fact, only 25–33% of psychotherapy clients are men (Rabinowitz & Cochran, 2002). Levant (1995) suggested the personal sharing and self-disclosure required in psychotherapy is foreign to many men, who have been taught since youth to avoid intimacy and vulnerability. *Alexithymia* refers to the inability to identify and talk about one's feelings, a condition widespread among the male population (Fischer & Good, 1997; Levant, 1995). Men are often encased in a "gender straightjacket," which is acquired at an early age and separates them prematurely and psychically from both "the loving connection of their mothers and from their inner voice of the warm and vulnerable parts of themselves" (Pollack, 2001, p. 541). Brooks (1998) explains that, as a result of these deficiencies, "Almost all men become highly dependent upon a woman to provide the intimacy and support that is so integral to their emotional well-being" (p. 39).

At one time it was thought that men experienced depression at only half the rate women did; however, more recent studies have shown that men experience depression at rates equal to that of women (Cochran, 2001). Depression in men is simply more likely to go undiagnosed and untreated, to manifest itself in alcohol or substance abuse, or worse, to end in suicide. Cochran stresses the importance of careful assessment for depression in men and the need to evaluate for comorbid conditions and alcohol or substance abuse, as well as the potential risk for suicide.

A men's support group as an intervention

When Toseland (1990) surveyed professional social workers, 80% of the respondents indicated that self-help groups are under-utilized by professional social workers. Kurtz and Powell (1987) listed six reasons why clinical social workers should encourage their clients to join self-help groups. These include increased social support, reduced dependency on significant others, opportunities to acquire and practice new skills, and developing positive self-perceptions and attitudes. According to Reddin and Sonn (2003), middle-aged men are particularly interested in connecting with each other for sharing and exploring meaning of life issues and dealing with personal growth and emotional difficulties. Richard (2000) stressed the need for clinicians to know how and when to recommend a men's support group as an adjunct to traditional counseling.

Difficulty in researching self-help groups and the current study

Some have indicated a difficulty in researching self-help groups. Levy (1976) pointed out that a myriad of self-help groups lack uniformity in rules and procedures, do not keep records, nor make any systematic attempt to assess their own effectiveness. Because self-help groups are not controlled by clinicians or researchers, studies of an experimental nature are practically non-existent (Lieberman, 1990). Lieberman (1990) reports that despite the overall positive findings in self-help groups, methodological problems of measurement and sampling have not permitted a definitive statement about their efficacy.

Magnuson (2007) suggests that not enough interview research or participant observation has been done, and scholars have been too focused on the textual analysis of popular mythopoetic writers such as Robert Bly. According to Mankowski (2000), we know relatively little about who participates in men's support groups, who benefits from them, and what, if any, changes men experience in their psychological well-being, their sense of purpose in life, their attitudes toward women, or their social life.

The current study looks at the effects of attending a men's support group. It focuses on the benefits for men in psychotherapy. To accomplish this, men were interviewed about their experiences in men's support groups and in psychotherapy.

Research methodology

The purpose of the current study is to explore participation in peer-led men's support groups to determine what men have to gain from these experiences. Specifically, the study focuses on the effect of regular concurrent attendance in a men's support group and how it might impact a man's experience of and work in psychotherapy.

Study design and sampling method

This is a qualitative study of data collected from the interviews of eleven men. The non-probability sample was selected on an availability basis within the Minneapolis and St. Paul metropolitan areas in the U.S.. The interviews were conducted using a semi-standardized format in which participants shared their demographic information and responded to questions about their background and experience in psychotherapy and men's support groups. All participants were middle-aged men, who within the past decade, had attended for a period of not less than three months both psychotherapy and a men's support group on a regular basis. Regular in both cases means not less than twice per month. The narrow sampling criteria preclude generalization of the findings.

Recruiting these men included two separate sampling strategies.

The first involved the Twin Cities Men's Center, where an invitation was posted on a bulletin board and also introduced in the open support group meetings hosted there over a period of one month. In addition, the facilitators were asked to provide a stack of invitations for attendees to pick up voluntarily, to which they could respond in private so as to preserve the privacy of their participation. The second strategy involved the wider community where privately held, closed support groups were identified and located through word-of-mouth leads. In other words, the researcher knew of men who participated in various support groups, and each of those men knew of other men who participated in other support groups, etc. When a group contact was made and approval was obtained, an introductory script was sent to invite participation in the study.

The interviewing process

All 11 participants were men of European descent, ranging in age from 38 to 65 years (M = 53.8, SD = 7.2), all American born citizens and long-time residents of the Minneapolis and St. Paul metro area. Educational backgrounds included two with high school only, one with trade school, three with B.A. degrees, three with MS or MA degrees, one Ph.D., and one M.D. All were employed in various professions with the following titles: civil engineer, property manager, photographer, gas station attendant, organizational consultant, massage therapist, program manager, mortgage banker, sales rep, contractor, and carpenter. Seven of the participants were currently married, six with children. Two were divorced, one of whom had children. Two had never been married.

Findings

The support groups represented in this study include the following: three separate open support groups at the Men's Center; an all male, open, Al-Anon group; three closed, independent men's support groups; and three closed I-groups (integration groups). Two participants were attending the same open group at the Men's Center, two others were attending the same I-group. The term *I-group* refers to generally closed support groups established by the Mankind Project (MKP), a worldwide men's organization dedicated to the development of integrity, authenticity, and compassion in relationships among men toward their families and communities (Mankind Project, 2010). The *I* represents the integration of relational skills learned by men who attend the *New Warrior Training Adventure Retreats* organized and operated by the Mankind Project.

Group size was very consistent among the closed groups. Of the six closed groups , five had eight members and one had six members. In contrast, the four open groups varied greatly in number with the average size ranging from 8 to 30. The sizes of the three open groups at the Men's Center were estimated by participants as a range, which varied considerably. The attendance in one of these groups varied from 6 to 20 participants, another varied from 3 to 14, and the third varied from 6 to 10. The open Al-Anon group, according to one participant, usually drew between 20 and 30 attendees.

Participants' histories in men's support groups

The average length of membership for the participants in their primary groups was 6.8 years, ranging from 1.5 to 27 years. The term *primary* is used because three participants were currently attending more than one support group. One was attending two groups, another was attending three groups, and a third was attending four groups. Each of these three participants identified a primary group to which they referred in response to the questions.

All but one participant had previously attended other support groups; six had been in two groups; four had been in three or more groups, and one of these men had been in 12 different groups. The total length of time these participants had been attending support groups in general ranged from 1.5 to 32 years (M = 15.6 years, SD = 10.7). Five of these men had attended support groups five years or less; five had attended support groups 25 years or more; one had attended support groups for 17 years.

Participants' histories in psychotherapy

All eleven participants had worked with more than one therapist in prior years. One participant had seen three therapists; two had seen two therapists each; four had seen four therapists each; two had seen eight therapists each; and one participant had seen 15 therapists. When asked how long they had been in psychotherapy and how long ago they had begun, all participants revealed long histories of psychotherapy. Regarding how long ago they began psychotherapy, the range was from 10 to 40 years ago (M = 25 years, SD = 7.1). For the total length of time each participant had attended psychotherapy, the range was 2 to 14 years (M = 8.6, SD = 3.2).

When asked about their most recent therapy, five participants said they were currently attending psychotherapy, four said they had seen their therapist within the past year, one said it had been two years prior, and another said four years prior.

The value and purpose of men's support groups

Social support and emotional support were among the most common benefit-reward themes, along with reduced isolation, fellowship, and community. All participants spoke of receiving social and emotional support. Three also spoke about giving support. One of the open-group participants gave this description of receiving emotional support:

> *There was a time when I was very depressed. I was talking about my wife taking the kids away and the hard time I was having dealing with her behavior, and I guess in my depression I started talking softer. Everyone was just leaning in closer to hear me, and I really felt a lot of support from that.*

The open-group participants all said they began attending support group meetings at a time of crisis in their lives. Three of them said this was typical. Here is an example of a crisis scenario one of these men described which motivated him to join a support group:

> *I found the support group when I was pretty much at the lowest point in my life, going through this surprise divorce and having some serious health*

issues that were all diagnosed at the same time, and feeling like everything around me had just evaporated, and I had nothing left. I'd never been through anything like that before, and then I found the support group, and it was a great help.

Reflecting on the supportive atmosphere in his group, one I-group participant said, "As I sit there sometimes and listen to other people, I realize this is profound; this is helpful; this is supportive."

Fellowship, community, and reduced isolation

Closely related to social and emotional support is the benefit of fellowship and community to which six of the participants referred. Three participants stated their belief that men tend to isolate themselves and that a men's support group is a good way to remedy that problem. One fellow put it like this:

[The support group] provides kind of a fellowship with peers. It's always helpful to hear the experiences of others... For a long time I was very isolated and kind of lost touch with what's appropriate behavior and what's not, how to even carry on a conversation, so meeting [with the] group has really helped me stay in touch with [a] community.

Another man pointed out what he called "a sense of connection to somebody else who has been or is going through something similar." Two others used *connection* as a term to describe the group experience, and two talked about why the connection became important to them. "I'm an only child," said one, "so it's always been challenging for me to feel like I'm part of a group, part of a clan, or part of a social structure, and [the group] gave me a lot of opportunity to build confidence around that." Another man said this:

I don't have any siblings. I had a brother, five years younger, who was killed in a car accident many years ago. These men have become my brothers, and we all feel that way toward each other. So there is a bond, there is a closeness.

One participant related his past experience of abuse to his tendency toward isolation:

[The support group] consistently calls me out of my isolation and loneliness. I grew up with six younger sisters in a family that...Well I'll put it this way, I grew up being bullied and beaten by my dad and other kids and grew up with a deep mistrust of other men and boys. So I isolated myself, TV, books, coin collection, did everything by myself. And to be in a men's support group is such a blessing for me.

Sharing, comparing, and a place to talk about feelings

Two participants spoke about the value of learning to talk about how they feel in front of the other men in the support group. Here is what one man said about this:

Until I started coming to this group, I really don't think I had much of an idea about how to talk about how I felt about just about anything. The group just made it less scary but also gave me a lot of practice at it. I really got a handle on what it's like to talk about how I feel, and to realize the benefit of doing that on a regular basis.

Another participant said, "It makes it easier for me to access my emotions when somebody right next to me is doing the same thing at the same level." One said this:

What it provides, [that] the individual counseling doesn't, is multiple peer perspectives, both questions and stories of experiences on a similar theme that often provide insight. [It] certainly helps provide a sense that I'm not the only one who is going through something, which is reassuring and educational.

Another commented on hearing from others. He said, "There's still something extra valuable about sitting down with other guys and actually hearing them tell their story."

Learning and skill building in the support group

These concepts were mentioned by at least half of the participants. The learning refers to instances when participants gained important knowledge about themselves or others, and the skill building refers to personal skills developed as a result of participation in the support group. An I-group member who had previously felt alienated from other men said, "In my support group, I actually now have a sense of what men are like [on the inside]… I gained that [knowledge] by being in men's support groups." Another fellow reported a social skill he learned in his support group. He said, "It [the support group] teaches me how to reach out better. It makes me not afraid to say, 'I'm having trouble; what should I do?'" Another participant credited his group for helping him to practice the social skills learned in the group in other settings.

> *It's been really interesting to take the skills [learned] from men's group and try them out comfortably [if] somewhat cautiously in other settings, with other friends, other family members, and certainly other business people. That's been a huge benefit of the men's group.*

Group issues: Anger and conflict resolution

Besides raising personal, family, and work issues in their groups, participants also revealed a variety of process and interpersonal communication issues involving anger and conflict. Four participants from the closed support groups reported experiencing conflict among the members. One said, "It gets very confrontational at times because we're very honest." Another put it like this:

> *You get the feeling of love and acceptance, and you also get the opportunity to have some disagreements. But it's a disagreement that doesn't change the underlying gift of the relationship, that I can risk being vulnerable enough to have an issue with you.*

Conflict was either less common in the open groups or less reported. Only two open-group participants reported conflict. One of these said,

"Rarely on occasion there are some people that rub you the wrong way, a very minor thing. I've never experienced any altercations or anything too alienating."

One of the closed I-group participants told of a conflict resolution strategy they employed routinely in which each partner of the conflict participates. It goes like this:

We use a five step model of conflict resolution. If there is conflict between two men, [1] what happened, [2] what is my perception about what happened, [3] what are my feelings about what happened, [4] what it reminds me of in my life, and [5] what I want going forward.

Comfort and safety in support groups

Four participants described a feeling of comfort and safety in their support group experience. For example, a member of an independent closed group said this:

[I] also just feel more of a warmth and support in the group. The therapy is more clinical...I don't think I've ever cried in front of a therapist. I can't get there. I can cry in front of these guys all the time. Yeah, it's much easier.

The other participant from that same group said, "There's a very high comfort level, very high safety, feeling of security or safety, because of the men you've been involved with for so many years." One of the I-group members offered this assessment: "There is touching and hugging. If necessary there is group hugging. There is supportive interaction that could never occur within the boundaries and limitations of the professional arena." The "professional arena" was a reference to psychotherapy.

Synergy between psychotherapy and men's support groups

Several of the interview questions targeted the participant's experiences in psychotherapy. The following four themes emerged from the responses: benefits and services received in psychotherapy; the relationship with the therapist and sentiments toward psychotherapy; the issues dealt with in psychotherapy; and what was gained or learned from psychotherapy. The details regarding these themes and examples of the responses are too numerous to include here.

Throughout the data analysis, ways in which men's support groups augment and reinforce psychotherapy became apparent, lending support to the hypothesis that a beneficial effect indeed results from concurrent participation in the two activities.

Six participants spoke about the support group reinforcing the therapy, and five spoke of the therapy reinforcing the support group. In the following comments, the support group appeared to reinforce the psychotherapy. One participant said, "[My support group] is a place to talk about what I learned in therapy and get reinforcement for it." Similarly, another participant said, "I probably [learned] more in individual therapy and then used the men's support group to build on that understanding and awareness." A third participant put it this way:

I was dealing with some things where there was a sense of anguish in talking about them initially. I would kind of test the waters in therapy first and then, as I gained more confidence, bring it to the men's support group... The support group in some ways really allowed me to put flesh on the bones that I created in therapy. It allowed me to flesh it out and make it real and bring it alive because it was done through relationships. So I was testing the benefits of my therapy in my support group through those relationships. It was a safe place to go back and talk about dissociation, what it felt like.

A fourth participant probably put it best with this description:

My therapist has given me the mechanics to appreciate the direction my life is going, but the men's group has given me the support, the guidance, the nurturing, the caring, the feeling, the ability to process or to role play that allows me to support this thrust.

One of the interview questions asked participants to identify ways in which the men's support group experience affected their progress in psychotherapy. One participant actually gave some credit to his support group for getting him into therapy. He said this:

In some ways [the men's Al-Anon group] made it possible for me to go to therapy because it removed the prejudice that real men don't do therapy. A whole lot of men in that group have gone to therapy, and so they model that, and they make it a lot easier to do therapy because there's such an acceptance of that in the group.

Another man gave credit to his support group for inspiring him to deal with certain issues in psychotherapy. He said, "Sometimes I [go] to a therapy with an issue I discussed in the support group, and I need to go further into it or need further help with the issue."

Effectiveness of psychotherapy versus effectiveness of support group

The interviews produced plenty of comparisons between psychotherapy and the men's support group experiences. Among many comments regarding these preferences and opinions, there appeared to be a rough balance between those who found the men's support group experience to be more valuable and those who found psychotherapy more valuable. Each participant was asked which he would choose if he had to choose between psychotherapy and his men's support group. Five men said they would choose their support group, three said they would choose psychotherapy, and three were noncommittal because they found both to be equally valuable. One participant said, "I don't think it's really that simple to choose one way or the other."

Conclusions and limitations

The main purpose of this study was to determine the effect of regular concurrent attendance in a men's support group on a man's work in psychotherapy. The findings support the hypothesis that a men's support group can be a beneficial influence on a man's progress in psychotherapy, which reinforces the Williams and Myer (1992) case study. The findings also reveal beneficial reciprocal effects of men's support groups and psychotherapy.

An obvious limitation of the current study is the small sample size, its self selection, and the lack of cultural and racial diversity in the sample which restricts generalization of the study's findings. The demographic mix was actually in line with existing men's movement literature. There could have been more effort to locate other racial or religious groups such as one might find in Christian Promise Keepers or possibly ethnic community centers.

The findings of this study have important implications for clinical social work practice in regard to the benefits and progress a man can achieve in psychotherapy and in men's support groups. More clinical social workers and other therapists should know about the potential advantages for male clients when they participate in men's support groups. It is important to know where a man can go to participate in a support group and what kind of interactions they can expect in the various groups available. If someone wants to join a closed group, the Mankind Project would be a good place to start. The MKP offers the weekend training known as the New Warrior Training Adventure, which prepares men to enter an I-group. See www.mankindproject.org.

Beyond simply referring a client to a men's support group, it is also important for the psychotherapist to know how to capitalize on the men's support group when a client is attending one. As several participants indicated, there is value in taking the skills learned in therapy and practicing them in the men's support group or at least discussing them in the group. Therapists could encourage male clients to practice self-disclosure, for example, in the support group. It is one thing to learn from the therapist but another thing altogether to put it to use with one's peers. A men's support group is one way to assist the client in removing the "gender straightjacket" suggested by Pollack (2001).

References

Barton, E. R. (2000). Parallels between mythopoetic men's work / men's peer mutual support groups and selected feminist theories. In E. R. Barton (Ed.), *Mythopoetic perspectives of men's healing work: An anthology for therapists and others* (pp. 3-20). Westport, CT: Bergin & Garvey.

Brooks, G. R. (1998). *A new psychotherapy for traditional men.* San Francisco, CA: Jossey-Bass.

Cochran, S. V. (2001). Assessing and treating depression in men. In G. R. Brooks & G. E. Good (Eds.), *The new handbook of psychotherapy and counseling with men.* (pp. 229-245). San Francisco, CA: Jossey-Bass.

Comstock, C. M., & Mohamoud, J. L. (1990). Professionally facilitated self-help groups. Benefits for professionals and members. In T. J. Powell (Ed.), *Working with self-help.* (pp.177-188). Silver Spring, MD: NASW Press.

Fischer, A. R., & Good, G. E. (1997). Men in psychotherapy: An investigation of alexithymia, intimacy, and masculine gender roles. *Psychotherapy, 34*(2), 160-170.

Kauth, B. (1992). *A circle of men: The original manual for men's support groups.* New York: St. Martin's Press.

Keen, S. (1991). *Fire in the belly: On being a man.* New York, NY: Bantam Books.

Kurtz, L. F., & Powell, T. J. (1987). Three approaches to understanding self-help groups. *Social Work with Groups. 10*(3): 69-80.

Levant, R. F. (1995). Toward the reconstruction of masculinity. In R. F. Levant & W. S. Pollack (Eds.) *A new psychology of men.* (pp. 229-251) New York,j NY: Basic Books.

Levy, L. H. (1976). Self-help groups: Types and psychological processes. *The Journal of Applied Behavioral Science, 12,* 310-322. Retrieved September 8, 2009, from Illiad.

Lieberman, M. A. (1990). A group therapist perspective on self-help groups. *International Journal of Group Psychotherapy, 40*(3), 251-278. Retrieved September 8, 2009, from Illiad.

Liebman, W., (1991). *Tending the fire: The ritual men's group.* St. Paul, MN: Ally Press.

Magnuson, E. (2007). *Changing men, transforming culture: Inside the men's movement.* Boulder, CO: Paradigm Publishers.

Mankind Project. (2010). *Our vision, mission, purpose, and values.* Retrieved March 19, 2010, from http://mankindproject.org/our-vision-mission-purpose-values.

Mankowski, E. S. (2000). Restructuring masculinity: Role models in the life stories of men's peer mutual support group members. In E. R. Barton (Ed.), *Mythopoetic perspectives of men's healing work: An anthology for therapists and others.* (pp. 100-117). Westport, CT: Bergin & Garvey.

Miller, J.E. (1998). *Effective support groups.* Fort Wayne, IN: Willowgreen Publishing.

National Institute of Mental Health. (NIMH, 2009). *Suicide in the U.S.: Statistics and Prevention.* Retrieved September 21, 2009 from http://www.nimh.nih.gov/health/publications.

Pollack, W. S. (2001). Masked men: New psychoanalytically oriented models for adult and young adult men. In G. R. Brooks & G. E. Good (Eds.), *The new handbook of psychotherapy and counseling with men.* (pp. 527-543). San Francisco, CA: Jossey-Bass.

Rabinowitz, F. E., & Cochran S. V. (2002). *Deepening psychotherapy with men.* Washington, DC: American Psychological Association

Reddin, J.A., & Sonn, C.C. (2003). Masculinity, social support, and sense of community: The men's group experience in Western Australia. *The Journal of Men's Studies, 11*(2): 207-223.

Richard, D. J. (2000). The therapeutic status of the mythopoetic approach: A psychological perspective. In E. R. Barton (Ed.), *Mythopoetic perspectives of men's healing work: An anthology for therapists and others.* (pp. 157-179). Westport, CT: Bergin & Garvey.

Schopler, J. H., & Galinsky M. J. (1995). Expanding our view of support groups as open systems. *Social Work with Groups, 18*(1), 3-10. Retrieved August 26, 2009, from the Social Work Abstracts database.

Sternbach, J. (1990). The men's seminar: An educational and support group for men. *Social Work with Groups, 13*(2), 23-39.

Toseland, R. W. (1990). Social workers use of self-help groups as a resource for clients. *Social Work, 30*(3), 232-237.

Williams, R. C., & Myer, R. A. (1992). The men's movement: An adjunct to traditional counseling approaches. *Journal of Mental Health Counseling, 14*(3), 393-404.

Yalom, I. D. (2005). *The theory and practice of group psychotherapy* (5th ed.). New York, NY: Basic Books.

10

Group member engagement in domestic abuse treatment: A mixed-methods study of two urban programs

Michael Chovanec

Abstract: *Engaging men in the change process is a challenge in domestic abuse treatment. This mixed-methods study examined engagement of men in group treatment. The Group Engagement Measure (GEM) was completed at three points by facilitators, and interviews were conducted with facilitators and a subsample of men. Significant change in engagement scores was found in one of the programs. When asked what keeps men engaged in treatment, the majority of men reported motivation to learn and learning new things. They also identified the importance of hearing other members' stories as motivators for positive change. Research and practice implications are discussed.*

Keywords: *domestic abuse treatment, engagement, batterer intervention programs*

Introduction

Engaging abusive men in the change process is a major challenge for group workers in domestic abuse treatment. Without it, the treatment process that supports men towards positive non-abusive change never happens. While domestic abuse treatment appears to be effective in ending physical abuse for program completers (Eisikovits & Edleson, 1989; Gondolf, 1991, 1997, 2004; Rosenfeld, 1992; Tolman & Bennett, 1990), program dropouts continue to present a significant problem for programs, men's partners and the community with between 22%

to 99% of men dropping out of treatment (Daly & Pelowski, 2000). Court orders used to retain men in the treatment process report mixed results. The safety of women is threatened as they often remain with partners who enroll in domestic abuse programs expecting them to complete the program and no longer abuse them (Gondolf, 1988). Yet, dropouts are more likely to re-offend than program graduates (Dutton, 1986; Edleson & Grusznski, 1988; Gondolf, 1997b, 1999; Palmer, Brown & Barrera, 1992).

This paper will report on a multi-method study examining engagement in two urban domestic abuse programs (N=195). Engagement data was gathered through interviews with both men (n=14) and facilitators (n=8). In addition, the Group Engagement Measure (GEM, Macgowan, 2006) was completed by facilitators on group members three times over the course of treatment. The research questions included the following:

1. What factors impact engagement and how does it change overtime?
2. How does engagement impact completion and dropout?

Literature review

Research studies of treatment programs for domestic abuse have focused on treatment outcomes with little focus on engagement (Babcock, Green & Robie, 2004; Bennett & Williams, 2001; Eisikovits & Edleson, 1989; Gondolf,1997, 2004; Rosenfeld, 1992). Studies examining attrition have focused primarily on static descriptive variables. (Daly & Pelowski, 2000), providing few guidelines for group facilitators on how to engage men who are abusive in the change process.

A few studies have examined the change process from the abusive men's and or the facilitator's perspective (Brownlee & Chlebovec, 2004; Gondolf & Hanneken, 1987; Pandya & Gingerich, 2002; Scott & Wolfe, 2000; Silvergleid & Mankowski, 2006). For example, men report both challenging abusive behavior and support by facilitators was crucial in helping them change (Silvergleid and Mankowski, 2006). In a recent qualitative study (N=27) examining men's perspective on engagement, participation in group discussion was the strongest theme with no themes developed pertaining to facilitators (Roy, 2011).

The stages of change model (Norcross, Beutler & Clarikin, 1998; Prochaska, Norcross & DiClemente, 1994) from the addiction field has been applied to domestic abuse treatment (Begun, Shelley, Strodthoff & Short, 2001; Daniels & Murphy, 1997; Levesque, Gelles & Velicer, 2000; Murphy & Baxter, 1997; Scott, 2004). The model suggests men go through a series of five stages to change their abusive behavior including pre-contemplation, contemplation, preparation, action and maintenance. The model suggests interventions need to match the stage of change men are in. Men in the first stage of change, pre-contemplation, are most likely to drop out (Scott, 2004). However, the study and this model does not address how best to engage abusive men through the stages of change toward a non-abusive outcome.

More recently there have been efforts to increase engagement with abusive men through the application of Motivational Interviewing (MI) prior to treatment and in the early stages of treatment. Musser, Semiatin, Taft and Murphy (2008) in a study (N=108) using a two-session MI intake compared to a standard intake (control) found the MI pre-group intervention led to more constructive in-group behavior including greater compliance with Cognitive Behavioral Therapy (CBT) homework assignments, higher therapist ratings of the working alliance and more men reporting help-seeking outside of group. In a smaller but randomized controlled study (N=33), Kistenmacher and Weiss (2008) reported that the MI pre-group intervention led to demonstrated movement by men on the Stages of Change Scale and also reported a significant decrease in the extent they blamed their violence on external factors.

Methodology

This study used a mixed method approach to examine engagement at multiple levels, and to address a gap in the literature that tends to focus on one method, either qualitative or quantitative. The study proposal was reviewed and approved by the school's Institutional Review Board.

Research setting

Both programs used open-ended groups and provided group orientations. Program 1 was an 18-week group program using a psycho-educational format. They had 6 ongoing groups that serve approximately 474 men per year. Men entered the program monthly, first attending an orientation and afterwards being assigned to a group. Men then completed an intake with one of four facilitators shortly after beginning the group (See figure 1).

Program 2 was a 23-week program in two parts, first providing an education focused group for 11 weeks and then a process/therapy group for 12 weeks. They had two education groups and 6 process/therapy groups that serve approximately 400 men per year. Men entered the program twice a month, first attending orientation and then completing an education focused group before completing an intake with one of the facilitators of the process group they were assigned to (See figure 1).

Figure 1
Treatment Process

Program 1 (18 weeks) — orientation---intake---psycho-education
Program 2 (23 weeks) – orientation – education group – intake – process group

Data collection

The study followed men who entered both programs with either monthly (Program 1) or bi-monthly (Program 2) orientations from January through April of 2009. Men were asked for their participation to be interviewed and if interested, interviews were conducted between sessions 3 and 6. During this time frame four full time facilitators from each program were interviewed as well. Both men and facilitators were paid $25 each for their interviews. For program 1, facilitators completed an intake with men after orientation and before group to gather demographic information and further orientate them to the program. For program 2, intakes were completed with the men by facilitators after the education focused group (11 weeks) and before the therapy/process group. Facilitators were also asked to complete the Groupwork Engagement Measure (GEM-27) on each group member that was assigned to their treatment group. Facilitators did not have knowledge of which group members were participating in the study. They completed this measure on all of their group members at three points in time (Between session 3-4, 6-12 and > 12 sessions).

Instruments

The Interview schedule was modified from an earlier qualitative study examining both facilitators and group members perception of engagement with involuntary groups (Levin, 2006). The schedule for the men consisted of 11 questions examining anger of men entering the program, the factors that impact their engagement in the group and where they see themselves in the process of change. The schedule for facilitators consisted of 9 items and assessed anger facilitators identified in the men, factors impacting men's engagement in group and a question asking how men's past trauma history impacts their ability to engage in group and reduce their abusive behavior. The schedule was reviewed by experts and professionals in the field.

The Groupwork Engagement Measure (GEM) was originally developed for facilitators to evaluate individual group members' level of engagement in close-ended treatment groups (Macgowan, 2006). It has 27 items that assesses seven dimensions of group engagement including attendance, contributing, relating to worker and with members, contracting and working on own and others' problems. Responses to the items are rated on a five-point Likert scale with higher scores indicating greater engagement. It has been used with a variety of closed and open-ended groups working with chemical dependency clients (Macgowan, 1997), sex offenders (Levenson, Macgowan, Morin

& Cotter, 2009) and mandated parenting and abuse groups (Levin, 2006). In regards to reliability, internal consistency across three studies reports excellent coefficient alphas (.97) with a desirably low standard of error of measurement of 4.52 for one study. Test-retest reliability was assessed in one study reporting a significant correlation (r [80] =.66, p<.001). Three measures across two studies used to determine criterion validity were moderately to highly correlated with the GEM (Macgowan, 2006).

Data analysis

The SPSS statistical program was used in the quantitative analysis of the data generated from the study (George and Mallery, 2006; Field, 2009). Descriptive analyses were conducted on all demographic information and scores on the engagement measures. Paired Sample T-tests were conducted comparing the same group of men's engagement scores over three points in time to determine the statistical significance of the changes in scores and an effect size was computed. In addition, completers and dropouts were compared on engagement scores using independent t-tests to check for significant differences between completers and dropouts.

Interviews for both facilitators (n=8) and group members (n=14) were audio-taped and transcribed and analyzed inductively using a content analysis (Berg, 2004). Open coding was conducted identifying themes generated for each question. Two or more participants identifying a similar code were considered a theme.

To address bias of the researcher, the research assistant also reviewed the transcripts separately and identified codes that represented participants' responses to questions. Codes identified were compared between researcher and assistant, with only similar codes used to identify themes for each question. Themes for each program were then compared and common themes were identified.

Table 1
sample characteristics / facilitators

Characteristic	Program 1	Program 2
Practice Experience (MN)	12 years	9 years
Gender	All female	1 female
		3 males
Ethnicity	All Caucasian	All Caucasian
Professional Licenses	3 – LSW	1 - LMFT
	1 – LICSW	1 – LPCC
		1 – LP in process
		1 – Not licensed

Findings

Program samples/facilitators

The majority of facilitators were seasoned professionals with an average of 12 years of practice experience Program 1 and 9 years for Program 2 (See Table 1). All of the facilitators were Caucasian and all except one were licensed or in the licensing process.

Program samples/men

Data was collected from two large urban domestic abuse programs, with a total of 95 men from Program 1 and 100 men from Program 2 entering each program from January thru April of 2009. The mean age for men was slightly older for Program 1 (Program 1 – 35; Program 2 – 33). Most men were court ordered with Program 2 having a slightly lower percentage of court ordered members (Program 1 – 97%; Program 2 – 88%). African American men represented the largest ethnic group in both samples (Program 1 – 51%; Program 2 – 39%). Caucasian men were the next largest ethnic group (Program 1 – 35%; Program 2 – 34%). Roughly half of the men were employed in both programs with Program 2 having slightly higher percentages of men who had completed Chemical Dependency Treatment and had identified with a mental illness (See Table 2). In Program 1 a significantly lower number of men responded to the questions about being physically abused or witnessing abuse.

Table 2
Sample characteristics / men

Characteristic (%)	Program 1 / n	Program 2 / n
Ever Arrested	93 (98) / 95	87 (95) / 91
Employed	36 (40) / 91	38 (52) / 91
Chemical Dependency Treatment	36 (39) / 93	34 (42) / 91
Mental Illness	31 (33) / 94	33 (40) / 91
Physically Abused	44 (75) / 59	22 (36) / 91
Witnessed Abuse	32 (64) / 50	34 (56) / 91
Living w/partner	29 (33) / 88	22 (29) / 91

In regards to attrition, Program 1 had 45% of the men dropout and Program 2 had 50%. Including repeaters in the analysis of attrition, roughly one third of the men in both programs were repeaters (See Table 3).

Table 3
Attrition rates including repeaters

	Program 1 N=95	Program2* N=99
Completers (%)	39 (41)	31 (31)
Repeat/Complete (%)	13 (14)	18 (18)
Repeat/Dropout (%)	21 (22)	19 (19)
Dropout (%)	22 (23)	31 (31)

* Program2 had one man who had dropped out and recently re-entered the program.

Engagement / facilitator perspective / scores

The Group Engagement Measure (GEM) was completed for 82 men in Program 1 and 39 men in Program 2. In Program 1 the GEM was completed by facilitators two to three group sessions after orientation. In Program 2 the GEM was completed by facilitators 10 to 13 sessions after orientation. The initial mean score of the GEM for Program 1 was 20.13 (SD=5.43) with a range of 9.1 to 32.2. For Program 2 the initial mean score was 25.05 (SD=5.47) with a range of 13.4 to 34.8.

In examining engagement scores over time both programs showed an increase in engagement overtime (See Table 4). In addition there was significant change overtime in program 1 but not in Program 2. There was statistically significant change in scores in Program 1 from time 1 to time 2 (t=-5.874, p=.00, 2-tailed), from time 2 to time 3 (t=-2.901, p=.00, 2-tailed) and from time 1 to time 3 (t=-5.695, p=.00, 2-tailed). The effect size for Program 1 (1.39) was approximately twice that of program 2 (.7). The changes in engagement scores for Program 2 were not statistically significant.

Table 4
Group engagement scores overtime

	Time 1	Time2	Time3
Program 1(n)	(82)	(59)	(34)
Mean	20.13	24.62	27.70
Standard Deviation	5.43	5.61	4.73
Program 2 (n)	(39)	(21)	(10)
Mean	25.05	26.75	28.92
Standard Deviation	5.47	5.21	6.74

In comparing initial engagement mean scores between completers and dropouts, both programs had higher mean scores for completers than for dropouts (See Table 5). In Program 1 the difference in mean scores between completers and dropouts came close to being statistically significant (t=1.85, p=.069, 2-tailed). Program 2 had a significant drop in sample size from completers to dropouts.

Table 5
Comparing engagement mean scores between completers and dropouts

	Completers	Dropouts
Program 1 (n)	(49)	(33)
Mean	21.00	18.85
Standard Deviation	5.68	4.84
Program 2 (n)	(34)	(5)
Mean	25.53	21.78
Standard Deviation	5.46	4.76

Engagement / themes

In this study all the facilitators from both programs and a subset of men (Program 1- $n= 8$; Program 2- $n=6$) were interviewed from both programs. While the interviews included a range of questions examining factors anticipated to impact the early sessions of group treatment, only those questions pertaining specifically to engagement will be reported here. All quotes will be italicized.

Men were asked to identify what factors keep them coming back to the group. The strongest theme was "learning things and motivation to learn" (10 out of 14 men).

I'm learning the words like denial and defense mechanism. . . We have a thing that they call a daily log and they write down how many times you get angry or what happens on that and I was surprised that through a given day all the little things that can make you angry. . . . I thought that it's the little things that I been picking up on.

Facilitators also strongly validated this theme as well (5 out of 8 facilitators).

I think maybe they start, the men start to have some awareness that there are issues they want to work on, that they are responsible, that they want better relationships, that they want better lives, and that particularly they maybe begin to notice that some of these issues for them are not only in intimate relationships but in other relationships they have at work and with friendships.

Men and facilitators were asked to identify what facilitators do or say that support the change process for men. No themes across programs were developed in either group.

Men and facilitators were also asked to identify what they see group members saying or doing that supported the change process for men. The strongest theme across both programs was that other men's stories motivated them to change (8 out of 14 men).

I feel, actually they're doing the same, they've been through the same thing that I've probably been through, and the one difference that I could say is the age group, by me being the youngest in my class, and I can honestly say everybody is at least 15, so 20 years older than me that's in this class, and...and it's kind of a step up before I reach that age, to actually see them like this, and I could probably piss them off (inaudible) at least I caught myself in this class early, so (inaudible) already have the mentality of, I know what anger management is and I know how to control it.

Facilitators also echoed this theme (5 out of 8 facilitators).

I think when they can talk about what resonates with them in other men's stories, and by resonate I mean what are they hearing that has a part that they have had an experience with, and what is it that they're hearing that's helpful or inspiring to them, and how can they take what they're hearing and bring that into their own lives.

In addition all of the facilitators voiced the importance of support and many identified challenge (5 out of 8 facilitators) as what they observed between group members. One facilitator, in recognizing the support exchanged between group members said:

A lot of time it's the in group support, resource sharing, how they've made change; but we also talk about who's the outside group facilitator, because oftentimes when they go out on break they're still talking about what happened in group or things they disagree with and why, and, you know, they may not be willing to say it to us, but they'll say it to the other guys.

Another facilitator in articulating the importance of men challenging each other said:

The most helpful thing that guys do, I think, is when they're able to say, I did what you did and I was exactly where you are and this was how I changed; and this just doesn't have to be veteran group members--excuse me--often it can be, but it takes all of the ammunition out of the argument of the other person when they're able to be confronted compassionately, and it normalizes it for them.

Discussion

Sample

Facilitators were seasoned and licensed professionals. All facilitators were Caucasian while the largest ethnic groups in both programs were African American. This may have impacted the engagement process.

While the attrition rate of 45% in Program 1 and 50% in Program 2 is comparable to other studies in the field (Daly & Pelowski, 2000), it impacted sample size in the data analysis. While demographic data and engagement data were collected early in the treatment process for Program 1 (within 3 weeks), attrition impacted the ability to collect engagement data for Program 2 (> 11 weeks). Fewer cases was one of the factors that limited the ability to differentiate engagement scores overtime for Program 2.

Engagement /facilitator perspective / scores

This study contributed to the limited knowledge in the literature that examines engagement in domestic abuse treatment from the facilitator's perspective using the Group Engagement Measure (GEM). Levin (2006) used the instrument to confirm engagement with group members that were interviewed. The instrument has also been applied in a Substance Abuse Treatment Group to improve facilitator interventions (Macgowan, 2006b). The GEM has also been applied in sex offender treatment (Levenson, Macgowan, Morin & Cotter, 2009) and in a parent-centered HIV prevention program for Hispanic parents and their children (Prado, Pantin, Schwartz, Lupei & Szapocznik, 2006).

The GEM appeared successful in measuring the engagement process as evidenced by engagement scores increasing overtime and higher scores for completers than for dropouts in both programs. Program 1 found significant change in engagement scores overtime with an effect size of 1.39. This compares favorably with a meta-analysis of studies that measured treatment effect size with voluntary populations (Asay and Lambert, 1999). In work with those diagnosed with depression, for example, the effect size ranged from .65 to 2.15. For anxiety disorders the range was .22 to 2.10. Program 1's effect size was also in the midst of high attrition (45%). Engagement scores were higher for completers than dropouts and came close to statistical significance (t=1.85, p=.069, 2-tailed). The GEM has been found to be a predictor of completion in other studies. Macgowen (1997) reports in a sample of adults with alcohol problems (N=77) that facilitator reports of client's progress towards goal completion correlated with GEM scores. Macgowen (2000) in a study of graduate student stress reduction groups (N=86) also reported low range correlations with a standardized outcome measure.

Program 2 had higher initial engagement scores with less change overtime. This can be explained by the program design. As mentioned earlier, men were not measured for engagement until later in the program since the comparable process/therapy group did not start until over 10 weeks into the program.

Engagement themes

"Learning things and motivation to learn" (10 out of 14 men) was the strongest theme when men were asked what reasons they continued in group. This was echoed by 5 out of the 8 facilitators. This was stronger than the other anticipated theme of court order which 5 out of 14 men identified. This theme appears similar to the theme 'willingness to change' identified in Roy's (2011) qualitative study of 27 men in domestic abuse treatment who were asked about their motivation for group. This motivation to learn theme could also be the result of selection bias for those interviewed, in that the most motivated were most likely to participate in the study

The strongest theme men reported regarding what was most helpful to them from group members was 'Motivation to change from hearing other men's stories' (8 out of 14 men). This was also echoed by 5 out of 8 facilitators. This theme was also mentioned in an earlier qualitative study examining men's reported changes from domestic abuse treatment (Silvergleid & Mankowski, 2006). This theme suggests the importance of open-ended groups where 'veterans' telling their stories to those entering the program. Story telling is also linked to the social components of the brain that allow individuals to build connections with others (Cozolino, 2006, 2008). Cozolino suggests hearing and telling stories uses a number of areas of the brain, helps us adjust our memories and contributes to healing. In addition, the importance of men's stories suggests facilitators need to find ways of incorporating the story telling process into the group process both in terms of presenting curriculum and allowing men opportunities to share their own stories as they make efforts to change.

Implications for domestic abuse treatment

This study confirms the importance of engagement in domestic abuse treatment for at least one program. Despite high attrition (45%), significant changes in engagement overtime was found. Is there a way of refining the facilitators approach to the group members in order to improve engagement early in the treatment process? Macgowan (2003, 2006) suggests the GEM can be used to provide information to facilitators to increase their efforts to engage group members and improve group outcomes. The clinical practice literature regarding work with voluntary individual clients suggest early engagement is a key to successful outcomes (Howard, Kopta, Krause & Orlinsky, 1986). In fact if change is not reported by clients by the third session there is on average no improvement reported over the course of treatment (Brown, Dreis & Nace, 1999). Miller, Duncan and Hubble (2004) suggest using client feedback on engagement to improve therapy outcomes. Simple rating scales are completed by the client and reviewed with the therapist. For example clients are asked if they felt heard, understood and respected. The use of these rating scales and this information exchange have resulted in significant improvements in both client retention and outcome (Miller, Duncan, Brown, Sorrell and Chalk, in press). Could this process and these scales be translated into work with involuntary groups and specifically Domestic Abuse treatment? Future research is needed to examine the relevance of this process and these scales for application with domestic abuse treatment.

Limitations and recommendation for future research

Given the differences between programs, engagement was not measured at the same time in the treatment process. Thus engagement scores were measured later in the group process (>11 weeks) in Program 2 and were initially higher and increased less overtime, compared to Program 1. It is recommended that future research examine engagement using similar programs, which allows for engagement to be measured at the same point in time for both programs.

Attrition also reduced sample size over time. This is a common problem in domestic abuse treatment (Daly & Pelowski, 2000). However, if engagement is measured early in the treatment process, as in Program 1, attrition should have less impact.

The engagement instrument in this study focused on the facilitator's perspective. While qualitative data was collected through interviews, the use of a quantitative measure completed by the clients would offer another perspective. Gathering evaluation data from group members about their relationship with facilitators, using a rating scale instrument as suggested by Duncan and Miller (2004), offers another option.

Conclusion

The main purpose of the mixed-methods study was to examine engagement overtime from the men's perspective through interviews and the facilitators' perspective through the Group Engagement Measure (GEM). This study contributed to the limited knowledge in the literature that examines engagement early in the treatment process for men who batter. Its mixed-methods design allowed for an in-depth examination of engagement in two large urban domestic abuse programs. Significant change was found in engagement scores in Program 1 with an effect size of 1.39. This compares favorably to other clinical populations who suffer with depression and anxiety (Assay and Lambert, 1999). In examining engagement from both men and facilitators about what factors assisted men in continuing in treatment, the key theme of "learning things and motivation to learn" was identified by the men (10 out of 14 men) and echoed by the facilitators (5 out of 8 facilitators). In addition, the most important theme identifying what men found helpful from other group members was "motivated to change from hearing men's stories' (8 out of 14 men) and this theme was also echoed by facilitators (5 out of 8 facilitators). Further examination of the engagement process is recommended to reduce attrition and improve outcomes for the betterment of abusive men, their families and the community.

References

Asay, T. & Lambert, M. (1999). The empirical case for the common factors. In M. Hubble, B. Duncan, & S. Miller (Eds.) *The heart and soul of change: What works in therapy, Chapter 2. Washington D.C.:* American Psychological Association: Washington D.C

Babcock, J.C., Green, C.E. & Robie, C. (2004). Does batterers' treatment work? A meta-analytic review of domestic abuse treatment. *Clinical Psychology Review, 23*, 1023-1053.

Begun, A.L.,Shelley,G.,Strodthoff T., & Short, L. (2001). Nonconventional approaches for intervention in cases of spouse/partner abuse. In Robert A. Geffner and Alan Rosenbaum (Eds.). *Domestic violence offenders: Current interventions, research and implications for policies and standards, pp. 105-127,*. NY: The Haworth Press, Inc.

Bennett, L. and Williams, O. (2001). In Brief: Controversies and Recent Studies of Batterer Intervention Program Effevctiveness. VAWnet Applied Research Forum.National Electronic Network on Violence Against Women. Project of the National Resource Center on Domestic Violence, pp. 1-13.

Berg, B.L. (2004). Qualitative research methods for the social sciences (5th Ed.). Boston: Allyn & Bacon.

Brown, J., Dreis, S. & Nace, D.K. (1999). What really makes a difference in psychotherapy outcome? Why does managed care want to know? In M.A. Hubble, B.L. Duncan, and S.D. Miller (Eds.). *The Heart and Soul of Change: What Works in Therapy* (pp. 389-406). Washington D.C.: APA Press.

Brownlee, K. & Chlebovec, L. (2004). A group for men who abuse their partners: Participant perceptions of what was helpful. American Journal of Orthopsychiatry, *74*(2), pp. 209-213.

Cozolino, L. (2006). *The neuroscience of human relationships, Attachment and the developing social brain.* NY: W.W. Norton and Company, Inc.

Cozolino, L. (2008). *The healthy aging brain, sustaining attachment, attaining wisdom.* NY: W.W. Norton and Company, Inc.

Daly, J.E. & Pelowski S. (2000). Predictors of dropout among men who batter: A review of studies with implications for research and practice. *Violence and Victims, 15*(2), pp. 137-160.

Daniels, J.W. & Murphy, C.M. (1997). Stages and processes of change in batterers' treatment, *Cognitive and Behavioral Practice. 4*(1), 123-145.

Duncan, B.L. & Miller, S.D. (2004). *The heroic client: Principles of client-directed, outcome-informed therapy* (revised edition). San Francisco, CA: Jossey-Bass.

Dutton, D.G. (1986). The outcome of court-mandated treatment for wife assault: A quasi-experimental evaluation. *Violence and Victims, 1,* 163-175.

Edleson, J.L. & Grusznski, R.J. (1988). Treating men who batter: Four years of outcome data from the Domestic Abuse Project. *Journal of Social Service Research, 12*(1), 3-22.

Eisikovits, Z.C. & Edleson, J.L. (1989). Intervening with men who batter: A critical review of the literature. *Social Service Review, 37,* 385-414.

Field, A. (2009). *Discovering statistics using SPSS* (3rd Ed.). Thousand Oaks, CA: Sage.

George, D. & Mallery, P. (2006). *SPSS for windows step by step (6th Ed.).* Upper Sadldle River, NJ: Pearson Education, Inc.

Gondolf, E.W. & Hanneken, J. (1987). The gender warrior: Reformed batterers on abuse, treatment and change. *Journal of Family Violence, 2,* 177-191.

Gondolf, E.W. (1988). The effects of batterer counseling on shelter outcome. *Journal of Interpersonal Violence, 3*(3), 275-289.

Gondolf, E.W. (1991). A victim-based assessment of court-mandated counseling for batterers. *Criminal Justice Review, 16,* 214-226.

Gondolf, E.W. (1997). Expanding batterer program evaluation. In G.K. Kantor & J. Jasinski (Eds.), *Out of darkness: Contemporary research perspectives on family violence.* Thousand Oaks, CA: Sage.

Gondolf, E.W. (1997b). Patterns of reassault in batterers programs. *Violence and Victims, 12,* 373-387.

Gondolf, E.W. (1999). A comparison of reassault rates in four batterer programs: Do court referral, program length, and services matter? *Journal of Interpersonal Violence, 14,* 41-61.

Gondolf, E.W. (2004). Evaluating batterer counseling programs: A difficult task showing some effects and implications. *Aggression and Violent Behavior, 9,* 605-631.

Howard, K.I., Kapta, S.M., Krause, M.S. & Orlinsky, D.E. (1986). The dose-effect relationship in psychotherapy. *American Psychologist,* 41, 159-164.

Kistenmacher, B.R. & Weiss, R.L. (2008). Motivational interviewing as a mechanism for change in men who batter: A randomized controlled study. *Violence and Victims,* 23(5), 558-570.

Levenson, J.S., Macgowan, M.J., Morin, J.W. & Cotter, L.P. (2009). Perceptions of sex offenders about treatment: Satisfaction and engagement in therapy. *Sexual Abuse: A Journal of Research and Treatment, 21*(1), 35-56.

Levesque, D.A., Gelles, R.J. and Velicer, W. F. (2000). Development and validation of a stages of change measure for men in batterer treatment. *Cognitive Therapy and Research, 24(* 2), pp.175-199.

Levin, K.G. (2006). Involuntary clients are different: Strategies for group engagement using individual theories in synergy with group development theories. *Groupwork, 16*(2), 61-84.

Macgowan, M.J. (1997). A measure of engagement for social group work: The Groupwork Engagement Measure (GEM). *Journal of Social Service Research,* 23(2), 17-37.

Macgowan, M.J. (2000). Evaluation of a measure of engagement for group work. *Research on Social Work Practice, 10*(3), 348-361.

Macgowan, M. J. (2003). Increasing engagement in groups: A measurement-based approach. *Social Work with Groups,* 26(1), 5-28.

Macgowan, M.J. (2006). The Group Engagement Measure: A Review of Its Conceptual and Empirical Properties. *Journal of Group in Addiction and Recovery, 1*(2), 33-52.

Macgowan, M. (2006b). Measuring and increasing engagement in substance abuse treatment groups:

Advancing evidence-based group work. *Journal of Groups in Addiction and Recovery,* 1(2), 53-67.

Miller, S.D., Duncan, B.L., Brown, J., Sorrell, R., & Claud, D. (in press). Using outcome to inform and improve treatment outcomes. *Journal of Brief Therapy.*

Miller, S.D., Duncan, B.L., & Hubble, M.A. (2004). Beyond Integration: the Triumph of outcome over process in clinical practice. Psychotherapy in Australia. 10 (2), 2-19.

Murphy, C.M. & Baxter, V.A. (1997). Motivating batterers to change in the treatment context. *Journal of Interpersonal Violence, 12*(4), 607-619.

Musser, P.H., Semiatin, J.N., Taft, C.T., &and Murphy, C.M. (2008). Motivational interviewing as a pregroup intervention for partner-violent men. *Violence and Victims,* 23(5), 539-557.

Norcross, J.C., Beutler, L.E. and Clarikin, J.F. (1998). Prescriptive eclectic psychotherapy. In R. A. Dorfman (Ed.), *Paradigms of clinical social work (Vol. 2, Chapter 11)*, NY: Brunner/Mazel

Palmer, S.E., Brown, R.A. & Barrera, M.E. (1992). Group treatment program for abusive husbands: Long-term evaluation. *American Journal of Orthopsychiatry, 62(2)*, 276-283.

Pandya, V. & Gingerich, W.J. (2002). Group therapy intervention for male batterers: A micro-ethnographic study. *Health and Social Work, 27(1)*, 47-55.

Prado, G., Pantin, H., Schwartz, S.J., Lupei, N.S., & Szapocznik, J. (2006). Predictors of engagement and retention into a parent-centered, ecodevelopmental HIV preventive intervention for Hispanic adolescents and their families. *Journal of Pediatric Psychology, 31(9)*, 874-890.

Prochaska, J., Norcross, J. & DiClemente, C. (1994). *Changing for good*. NY: Avon Books.

Rosenfeld B. (1992). Court-ordered treatment of spouse abuse. *Clinical Psychology Review, 12*, 205-226.

Roy, V. (2011, June). Perceptions of men about their engagement in domestic abuse groups. Paper presented at the 33rd Annual International Symposium for the Association for the Advancement of Social Work with Groups, Long Beach, CA.

Scott, K.L. (2004). Stage of change as a predictor of attrition among men in a batterer treatment program. *Journal of Family Violence*, 19(1), pp.37-47.

Scott, K.L. & Wolfe, D.A. (2000). Change among batterers, Examining men's success stories. *Journal of Interpersonal Violence, 15(8)*, 827-842.

Silvergleid, C.S., & Mankowski, E.S. (2006). How batterer intervention programs work. *Journal of Interpersonal Violence, 21(1)*, pp139-159.

Tolman R & Bennett, L. (1990). A review of quantitative research on men who batter. *Journal of Interpersonal Violence, 5*, 87-118.

11

Harnessing the promise of diversity in group work practice

Robert Basso, William Pelech, and Edcil Wickham

Abstract: *This inquiry utilized a grounded theory approach to learn how practitioners conceptualize and use diversity in their groups. We found that there was general confusion about the term "diversity" among all respondents. Practitioners offered little on how one can strategically use diversity within a group to promote group development. They also noted some ambivalence about the benefits and challenges posed by diversity in groups. In working with diversity, practitioners suggested open discussion about the differences evident in the group. Further research into how practitioners can harness diversity in service of group development and therapeutic goals is clearly warranted.*

Keywords: *Diversity, group work, qualitative methods, social work*

Introduction

There is an increasing awareness of the need for culturally sensitive practice today because of the changing demographics in our communities. The changes arising from life in an increasingly globalized world have further reinforced a demand for more inclusive approaches to practice. However, there is limited research especially into group practitioners' understandings and roles in working with diversity. Honoring the rich interprofessional tradition in social group work, we set out to learn how practitioners from different professional orientations conceptualized diversity while attending to diversity in group work. We contacted group practitioners from pastoral counseling, psychology and social work professions to inquire about how these different professionals assist individuals and the collective to achieve their goals. We assumed that different professional orientations might have differing perceptions and conceptualizations which could inform the development of an approach or model useful for all of the professions.

Review of the literature

Diversity has been generally defined as the state or quality of being different, unlike in character or qualities. Definitions of diversity include "variety, unlike in nature" (Oxford Dictionary, 2001, p. 276) and "variety, or the opposite of homogeneity" (Barker, 2003, p. 126). Definitions also include descriptions of people from minority populations and people from varied backgrounds, cultures, ethnicity and viewpoints, a common orientation for many human service organizations. While the usage of the term diversity is more recent, group practice has always emphasized respect for the uniqueness of each individual and the importance of democratic values in practice. In the 1930's, at a time when social group work included professionals from a wide array of disciplines, Coyle (1930) realized that member differences bring creative potentials to a group. Many group practitioners since then have also realized the value and creative potential arising from the recognition and integration of differences (Newstetter, Feldstein, & Newcomb, 1938; Tropp, 1969; Konopka, 1956; Kaiser, 1958; Goroff, 1980, Kurland & Salmon, 1998, Phillips, 1957). Kurland and Salmon (1998) have delineated two major categories arising in groups: (1) descriptive or demographic dissimilarities in terms of racial, ethnic, cultural, gender or other member characteristics; and (2) differences of opinion or perspectives which also may arise as a result of diversity in the membership of a group. Summing up these notions, Helen Phillips (1957), citing Dewey (1934) affirmed how effective social work groups must demonstrate "unity in variety" (p. 144).

Although contemporary professions devote much attention to diversity, there is limited research into the role that diversity plays in group practice. More worrisome are the findings in one study suggesting that when faced with group members' differences, or working with members from different backgrounds, the most common response from group leaders was that they did nothing (Rittner, Nakanishi, Nackerud, & Hammons 1999). The findings of Davis, Galinsky and Schopler (1995) were also disquieting because they noted that practitioners working with multiracial groups expressed concerns that group members would perceive the leaders as having insufficient understanding of issues and would not participate in discussion due to racial tension or concerns about racist behavior or condescension.

In the psychology literature, Jackson, May & Whitney (1995) identified two sources of diversity in task-related groups, one based on demographic characteristics (e.g. age, gender, race, and nationality) and the other relating to other informational differences (e.g. perspectives, attitudes, values, socioeconomic and personal status, education, work experience, and personal expectations). Many researchers (Milliken, Bartel & Kurtzberg, 2003; Hoffman & Maier, 1961; McLeod, Lobel & Cox, 1996; Watson, Kumar, & Michaelsen, 1993) have observed that informational diversity in groups provides for greater variation in perspectives, enabling group members to develop different approaches to dealing with problems or issues and reach more complex, innovative and higher quality solutions. These observations may explain why heterogeneous groups have outperformed other interactive (homogenous or nominal) groups and generated more semantically diverse ideas than the others groups (Stroebe & Diehl, 1994). Miura & Hida (2004) have noted that diversity of ideas among the members leads to the sharing of numerous unique and varied ideas and thus to an enhanced creative potential for the group, supporting a value-in-diversity orientation. Diversity may also have a positive impact on the quality of final group outcomes by providing valuable resources (e.g., alternative viewpoints, a broader range of expertise, and other human capital assets) to be used in problem solving, decision making, and implementing activities.

Recent research suggests that multi-cultural groups develop more and better alternatives to a problem and criteria for evaluating those alternatives than do culturally homogeneous groups (McLeod, Lobel & Cox, 1996). Three studies offer evidence that there may be benefits in terms of the number of alternatives considered in a decision-making task and the degree of cooperation within the group that accrue to groups that are diverse with respect to race or ethnic background (Cox, Lobel & McLeod, 1991; McLeod, Lobel & Cox, 1996; Watson et al., 1993). In sum, given the growing demographic diversity that has occurred in our increasing globalized world and the abovementioned research findings, there is a clear and compelling need for a new and more inclusive model of group work practice.

Methodology

The goal of this project was to identify various professional practitioners' awareness, understandings, and uses of diversity as a central construct of group practice within the contemporary Canadian context. At the outset, we assumed that different professional training and preparation, different professional practice orientations, and historical practice connections to client groups might inform an interprofessional model of group practice.

Professional group leaders in community-based human service practice settings were recruited from agencies whose mandates are to provide direct services to clients with a variety of presenting problems. A total of seven counselors participated who were drawn from six different community-based organizations. Two were from psychology, one from pastoral counseling and four were from social work. Each of the group leaders had practiced a minimum of eight years.

Before asking our questions, each participant was invited to reflect on his or her practice experiences when framing his or her responses or elaborations. The questions we posed included: How do group leaders understand diversity as it occurs in their daily work? How aware are professionals about what diversity is and represents? What do professionals do with diversity? How well do practitioners recognize diversity as a part of everyday existence, problems and solutions? The opening questions set the stage for each group leader to elaborate on his or her perceptions of how diversity played into group progress. Personal interviews were digitally recorded with each group leader's permission.

As our research intent focused on constructing an interprofessional understanding of group leadership and practice applications, a grounded theory approach was utilized (Morse, 1994; Corbin, 2008; Charmaz, 2006). Initial creation of categories occurred in the analysis of the interviews using a constant comparative method. Pivotal to grounded theory is theoretical sampling or selection of participants on the basis of concepts that have proven theoretical relevance to the evolving theory (Strauss & Corbin, 1998). Thus, theoretical sampling led us to recruit practitioners from various professions who led a wide variety of groups. Statements emanating from the interviews were placed into groupings. These groupings served to create the basis of descriptive understandings of the uses of diversity across the life of groups.

Adopting a strategy similar to Wheelan and Hochberger (1996), categories were created, then data sorted that best fit within these categories. The results section demonstrates the data that ground the concepts. New categories emerged in the initial analysis of the diversity-focused discussions and consequently, additional characteristics emerged during analysis necessitating some recoding of data and concepts.

Results

Understandings of diversity

In answering the question "what is diversity?" we found that there is a universally demonstrated confusion about the term 'diversity' among all respondents from the different professional practice contexts. Respondents used the term to mean both heterogeneity within a group and differences between groups. The data shows that practitioners identified both differences among members in a group setting, and the differences in the society-at-large. Many times the group leaders would oscillate between the two.

Each of the respondents is identified by his or her professional affiliation in the quotes below, with SW (1-4) standing for social work, PS (1-2) representing psychology, and PC symbolizing pastoral counseling.

SW1: Okay, diversity (pause) is a phenomenon, um, that includes differences, which may involve disadvantage as well as advantage... And it by no means is to be relegated to cultural, uh,differences in society, but involves differences in society.

PS2: Huh. Uh, well everything from, uh... in terms of working with people? "I guess, um, I guess uh you know, looking at everything from, um, you know, everything from, uh, uh, the multi-cultural aspect and where they're coming from and respecting that to people with disabilities and also the, I don't know, the sexual orientation and so on.

PC: I guess, basically, different from what's considered mainstream, or any kind of differences within the group... So it could be everyone in the group is different in some way. Uh, whatever makes one unique or unique, or specific to the majority, that would be my understanding of, of diversity.

Respondents talked about diversity both referring to differences between their groups (e.g. different types or for specific populations) and within their groups. There is confusion among practitioners as to what diversity really is. The practitioners' examples indicate that they were not operating with a clear and practice-ready definition of diversity. The practitioners' understandings of aspects of diversity were always highlighted in the following taxonomy:

*   Physical (e.g., gender, age, skin color, and physical disabilities)
*   Psychological (e.g., mental illness, ways of thinking, and attachment)
*   Familial (e.g., orphan, marital status, and custodial/non-custodial parents)
*   Socioeconomic Status (e.g., wealth, profession, education, and literacy level)
*   Cultural (e.g., sexual orientation, language, religion, and nationality/ ethnicity)
*   Situational (e.g., mandated to attend group, and in prison)

The practitioners demonstrated a familiarity with some understanding of diversity and assumed it has implications for groups, yet were non-specific about impacts of diversity on practice.

Recruitment and group practice with diversity

Practitioners usually established groups by inviting potential members based upon a variety of commonalities, rarely if ever around differences. They had formed groups around as many commonalities as seemed appropriate, and their emphasis was on 'how persons are alike', and not how members bring 'who you are' to a group that encompasses differences. According to the practitioners, members are usually selected for groups based on presenting problems and are randomly allocated on a first-come-first-served basis. Although sometimes groups are designed to be heterogeneous (e.g., co-ed divorce group), diversity is often seen as an unavoidable reality that results from happenstance rather than through intentional planning.

SW1: In most of group programming, diversity is not how participants are selected. I'm not always sure we've paid attention to diversity unless it's been a specific population that's attending (gives example of Asian men's group).

PC: Members not selected into programs based on diversity characteristics - Some consideration is given about who goes into small groups, based on 'personality fit' but not diversity related characteristics.

PS2: Women aren't sought out for diversity, it's by happenstance...we used to screen for group fit but no longer do.

SW3: We do not use diversity oriented mechanisms to select members, we offer more compatible groups if programming allows - a mix and match method versus the first-come-first-served method of participant allocation.

Diversity in groups can sometimes be seen by practitioners as being a barrier to care that needs to be managed or eliminated. Some of the practitioners indicated that they were hesitant to admit individuals, if these potential members differed from the existing members in the group.

SW4: I've been fortunate as to have, uh, Aboriginal, uh, parents become involved in the screening process only to find out that their Aboriginal beliefs and framework weren't going to be suitable for the group.

PS2: Trying to respect same sex relationships and trying just talking a little with them and we don't have a same sex group, we just don't have the population, so asking them how they're going to feel about sitting in is all we can do.

Diversity as a challenge to the foundations of caring

Although diversity may be seen as an asset to a group, "Diversity is a gift, the differentness allows a different intensity of work for members" (SW2), there is an underlying discomfort with the differences among group members. Whether or not difference in a group can be an asset or liability in achieving therapeutic goals, there is no doubt that it is uncomfortable being the member who is different. People fear what the other members may think about them and may fear being rejected based on their past experiences:

> *PS1: A client brings in how the world has responded to his or her differentness and, and then that person would bring that into the group. For example, whether or not someone has spent time incarcerated or not and how other people would respond to finding that out, or not.... Or how much do I share about past experience, how much is relevant for me to share, uh, will it make other people feel safe or unsafe if they know this, is it relevant for them to know different kinds of past experiences in that regard.*

If clients view themselves as being different from the other members, they may choose to never enter the group in the first place, which is not only detrimental for the client, but also 'bad for business' (SW2). To make the organization's groups more appealing to diverse clients, agencies take steps to make clients more comfortable by either creating groups with common traits or by employing "diverse staff", which decreases rather than emphasizes diversity in the agency environment.

> *SW3: We don't want to be a 'WASPY' looking agency when offering services to newcomers. We recruit staff who speak different languages in an effort to bring multi-cultural elements in... such as with staff recruitment, trying to broaden staff with different languages, different backgrounds.*

> *PS2: "We don't want them running away screaming...*

In running groups, the professional staff discussed some challenges related to setting or achieving goals in diverse groups. These included the problem of outlining common goals, as well as helping diverse members build enough self-esteem to achieve their goals, especially if they believed they would be rejected because of their difference.

> *PC: I cannot imagine a group without diversity but see some challenges with diversity when group cannot agree on basic building blocks.*

> *SW3: Diverse groups are challenging...it's hard to find a common goal and hard to reach very different goals...goals need to be much more individualized...it's the difference of what people need and it's hard to reach and meet those diverse needs.*

PS1: I guess for a lot of people what makes them different has been a barrier to their success and so if they haven't felt supported in who they are, if people make assumptions about them that don't support them, um, that could make what they want to achieve difficult.

Language barrier: A challenge

Probably the most commonly cited challenge of diversity was language barriers including finding language appropriate materials. However, more frequently practitioners talked about the need for language interpreters to ensure the full participation of group members, including English interpreters as well as interpreters for the deaf.

SW3: It's hard...we have difficulty finding group materials that are language appropriate."

SW2: We have used interpreters in the past, we're open to interpreters to ensure someone's participation... including a deaf person once.

Practitioners' plans for working with diversity

The practitioners suggested, in order to deal with diversity, members should talk openly about the differences evident in the group.

SW2: We talk about differences from the very beginning...it's part of the group rules and procedures to discuss different backgrounds, different faiths..we talk about how differences are OK.

SW3: It's not so much the group is, is um, uh, has a problem with diversity, but the group becomes a place for diversity to become, uh, reviewed, talked about, expressed with people then. It's made okay.

PS1: So in our group rules I've never had a group where we haven't had guidelines for safety in the group, um, they always include a statement like no one should use language that would violate the dignity of any person in the group. So looking to ask group members not to be racist, not to be sexist, not to be homophobic, um, and then stating outright that we'll challenge those statements, and inviting other people to challenge language that would be hurtful.

PS2: The leader has to do modeling for other people... how to challenge respectfully and challenging people in a way that's respectful, that doesn't violate their dignity.

PC: Sometimes you just have to see the diverse persons in a one-to-one situation away from the group..The leader tries to reach the majority of the group, using tools, language, content that most can use.

SW1: Well, consciousness of language would be important. So for example, using a term um like partner rather than spouse or wife or girlfriend or boyfriend, partner is very respectful because it could include all of those relationships.

SW4: Then we move to diversity and do we make accommodation, we had to, uh, in regards to the Aboriginal woman to the point where I... consulted with my group about whether she'd need to do ceremony.

Finally, practitioners spent a great deal of time talking about understanding the clients. This seemed to be a very important point as it was brought up repeatedly throughout the interviews. The most common piece of advice given is to take time to learn about and really listen to the clients, and try to see the world through their eyes.

SW4: Always check into the world of, of the one with the difference, with the diversity as to their world rather than assume that we know... different lands, different ways of being, different patterns, different expectations... we have to enter into the world of children and of parents that we're working with, uh, to understand what their goal process will be. It's not necessarily North American, for example, our ways in which we grieve are very different than, than, uh, other countries around the world.

PS1: Um, how do different ethno-cultural communities learn? How do they communicate with each other? What's their history of getting information or of sharing information with each other? If we don't know that then our way that we traditionally do things may not be effective at all. So finding out what is going to be, what will positively resonate with different kinds of communities and different kinds of people, seeking them out, going to where they will be instead of just assuming they'll find us, um, if they need us they'll find us, that's probably not a good attitude to have. Um, finding out where they are and making sure that they have the information in a way that will be useful to them, that would be helpful.

Discussion

Despite the recognition of diversity as a potential resource for assisting the group in achieving tasks and goals (Sullivan, 2004), practitioners offered very little commentary on how one can strategically use diversity within a group to either promote group development, cohesion or achievement of therapeutic goals. Indeed, evident in their responses was some ambivalence about the benefits and challenges posed by diversity in groups. On one hand, the group leaders acknowledged the importance of exploring differences expressed among group members, a practice concept noted by Kurland and Salmon (1998). Most believed that with a diverse group, practitioners might build on the strengths of diversity to enhance problem solving. They also see diversity as something that is needed to have productive groups, as various perspectives enrich challenging encounters. On the other hand, paralleling the past treatment of diversity in the literature, group leaders thought that diversity should be "accommodated" and that diverse members may choose not to enter, feel uncomfortable in a group context, or simply drop out when a group has not been specifically designed to meet their needs. (Rittner et al., 1999). Overall, the group leaders valued diversity as an ingredient that is necessary for productive groups, as the members' various perspectives can enrich challenging encounters.

These findings are limited by the number of practitioners who participated in this in-depth qualitative study from one country. Seven participants is a relatively small number for studies utilizing grounded theory. Consequently, we cannot infer that these findings are representative of group work practitioners in general. We have attempted to offer a credible interpretation of participant responses through providing examples of participant statements. However, our interpretation will be influenced by our standpoint and concerns about group work practice. We hope that these tentative findings will contribute to conversations and further research into how diversity can be harnessed in service of group development and therapeutic goals.

Conclusions

The context of practice has changed in the past half century since the emergence of helpful group models, such as the Tuckman (e.g., "forming" "storming" etc.) or the Boston models. The globalized world has numerous facets that may not fit into models created almost half a century ago. Groups did not then have to cope with as many of the elements of diversity as seen today. Extreme differences now exist at the neighborhood level and these differences will be reflected in every human group.

The seasoned practitioners from various professional backgrounds had difficulties describing their utilization of diversity. All of the professional group leaders expressed similar struggles with diversity in practice. According to the group leaders' inputs, the professions are also wrestling with these issues. Although they recognized that a group member's world view provides a group with some unique opportunities for members to give meanings to their experiences and informs their ways of relating to others (Anderson, 1997), they acknowledged that there is a need for further theoretical development i.e. the creation of a "blueprint" for assisting individuals, group leaders, and human service organizations to deal with diversity and to create successful group development.

Effective group functioning depends upon a leader who is skilled at recognizing diversity in order to assist the group in its progress towards goal achievement. Individual members need assistance in formulating their personal goals. These are then achieved by working towards the group's purpose and goal attainment. Effective group functioning will yield opportunities for goal attainment. Effective practice can be seen to mean effective group problem solving, and groups that deal with diversity are more likely to develop skills in problem solving. In this way, leaders and members in organizational, community and international contexts will also potentially benefit from this research. As Towle (1965) identified in *Common Human Needs*, people's psycho-social needs are tied to diverse and complex life experiences.

She advocated that practitioners attend to assisting the clients to work together in order to achieve their common needs. In sum, it would appear that some of the early assumptions about the importance of homogeneity and commonalities in group work which underpin our early group practice models may only offer partial direction to group leaders today. The harnessing of diversity may need to be developed earlier in the life of a group. As DeLucia-Waack and Donigian (2004) have observed, perhaps real cohesion arises out of shared experiences among group members, and that the differences between group members be explored sooner. Members of the interprofessional community have a role to play in this future model development.

References

Anderson, J. (1997). *Social work with groups: A process model.* New York: Longman.

Barker, R. (Ed.) (2003) *The social work dictionary (5th ed.).* Washington, D.C.: NASW Press.

Charmaz, K. (2006). *Constructing grounded theory.* London: Sage.

Corbin, J. (2008). *Basics of qualitative research: Techniques and procedures for developing grounded theory.* (3rd ed.). Los Angeles: Sage.

Cox, T. H., Lobel, S. A., & McLeod, P. L. (1991). Effects of ethnic group cultural differences on cooperative and competitive behavior on a group task. *Academy of Management Journal, 34,* 827-847.

Coyle, G. (1930). *Social processes in organized groups.* New York: Richard R. Smith.

Davis, L., Galinsky, M., & Schopler, J. (1995). RAP: A framework for leadership of multiracial groups. *Social work, 40* (2), 155-165

Delucia-Waack, J. & Donigian, J. (2004). *The practice of multicultural group work.* Belmont, CA: Brooks/Cole.

Dewey, J. (1934). *Art as experience.* New York: Berkley Publishing Group.

Goroff, N. (1980), Social group work: An intersystemic frame of reference. In A. Alissi (Ed.), *Perspectives on social group work practice* (pp. 292-303). New York: The Free Press.

Henry, S. (1981). *Group skills in social work.* Itasca, Ill: Peacock Publishers.

Hoffman, L. & Maier, N. (1961). Quality and acceptance of problem solutions by members of homogeneous and heterogeneous groups. *Journal of Abnormal Social Psychology, 62,* 401-407.

Jackson, S. E., May, K. E. & Whitney, K. (1995). Understanding the dynamics of diversity in decision-making teams. In R.A. Guzzo, E. Salas, et al. (Eds.), *Team effectiveness and decision-making in organizations* (pp. 204-261). San Francisco: Jossey-Bass.

Kaiser, C. (1958). The social group work process. *Social Work, 3*(2), 67-75.

Konopka, G. (1956). The generic and the specific in group work practice in the psychiatric setting. *Social Work, 1*(1), 73-80.

Kurland, R. & Salmon, R. (1998). *Teaching a methods course in social work with groups.* Alexandria VA: Council on Social Work Education.

McLeod, P., Lobel, S., & Cox, T. (1996). Ethnic diversity and creativity in small groups. *Small Group Research 27*(2), 248-264.

Milliken, F. Barel, C. and Kurtzberg, T. (2003). Diversity and creativity in work groups. In P. Paulus & B. Nijstad (Eds.). *Group creativity: Innovation through collaboration.* (pp. 32-62). New York: Oxford University Press.

Miura, A. & Hida, M. (2004). Synergy between diversity and similarity in group-idea generation. *Small Group Research, 35*(5), 540-564.

Morse, J. (1994). Designing funded qualitative research. In N. Denzin & Y. Lincoln, *Handbook of qualitative research.* (pp. 220-235). Thousand Oaks CA: Sage.

Newstetter, W., Feldstein, M., & Newcomb, M. (1938). *Group adjustment: A study in experimental sociology.* Cleveland: School of Applied Social Sciences, Western Reserve University.

Northen, H. (1988). *Social work with groups.* (3rd ed.). New York: Columbia University Press.

Oxford Dictionary, (2001). London: Oxford University Press.

Phillips, H. (1957). *Essentials of social group work skill.* New York: Association Press.

Rittner, B., Nakanishi, L., Nackerud, L., & Hammons, K. (1999). How MSW graduates apply what they have learned about diversity to their work with small groups.

Journal of Social Work Education, 35(3), 421-431.

Stroebe, W. & Diehl, M. (1994).Why groups are less effective than their members: On productivity: Losses in idea-generating groups. *European Review of Social Psychology, 5,* 271-304.

Strauss, A., & Corbin, J. (1998). *Basics of qualitative research: Techniques and procedures for developing grounded theory* Thousand Oaks, CA: Sage.

Sullivan, N. Conflict as an expression of difference: A desirable group dynamic in anti-oppressive social work practice. In C. Carson, A. Fritz, E. Lewis, J. Ramey, & D. Suguichi (Eds.), *Growth and development through group work*. (75-89). New York: Haworth Press.

Towle, C. (1965). *Common Human Needs*. New York: National Association of Social Workers.

Trecker, H. (1972). *Social group work*. New York: Association Press.

Tropp, E. (1969). *A humanistic foundation for group work practice*. New York: Selected Academic Readings.

Watson, W., Kumar, K., & Michaelsen, L. (1993). Cultural diversity's impact on interaction process and performance: Comparing homogeneous and diverse task groups. *Academy of Management Journal, 36*, 590-602.

Wheelan, S. & Hochberger, J. (1996). Validation studies of the group development questionnaire. *Small Group Research, 27(1)*, 143-170.

Index

Note: the letter 'f' following a page number refers to a figure; the letter 't' refers to a table.